To Anne-Marie with love

till time and times are done

ACS cleaning lustre pots, 1991.

Photography of Alan Caiger-Smith pots by Jon Atkinson.
Design by Suzy Gallina.
Production by Wendy Wort.
Print and Reproduction by Flaydemouse, Yeovil, England.
Published by Richard Dennis, The Old Chapel, Shepton Beauchamp, Somerset TA19 0LE.
© Alan Caiger-Smith and Richard Dennis
ISBN 0 903685 39 6
All rights reserved
British Library Cataloguing-in-Publications Data. A catalogue record for this book is available from the British Library.

POTTERY, PEOPLE AND TIME

A Workshop in Action

by

Alan Caiger-Smith

RICHARD DENNIS
1995

ACKNOWLEDGEMENTS

First and foremost I thank Giles de la Mare for an idea that led, in the course of time, to something that neither of us could clearly foresee. He put steel to my flint, kindling the fire that eventually lit up the themes of these chapters.

I am grateful to the Elmgrant Trustees, Dartington, for their interest in the book at an early stage and for their financial assistance when the future seemed to hold only dust and ashes. Equally I thank Willem van de Loo for his generous, personal financial help and for his enthusiastic response to an early version of the text.

Amongst a number of supportive friends, I thank David Castillejo especially, for his sustained appreciation of the idea from the very beginning, for his insight into what had been done and for showing me what was still lacking.

I am indebted to Clare Cherrington for her critique of the material and my writing, for her cautions and her detailed positive suggestions. I have tried to put most of her advice into effect and know that I deviate from it at my peril.

My thanks are due also to the potter Dani le Hardy of South Carolina for her encouragement and for a quantity of solicited and unsolicited photograph illustrations. For other illustrations and for kindly support I thank Jonathan Kingdon, Julian Bellmont, Laurence McGowan, Kristine Michael, Nicholas Caiger-Smith, Madeleine Dinkel, Jan de Rooden, Ruth Duckworth, Antonia Salmon and Kenneth Clark, and I thank David Leach for his trust and helpful advice.

I acknowledge kind permission to quote from publications within their copyright from William Collins Son and Co. Ltd, Faber and Faber Ltd, the Trustees of The South Bank Centre, London, The Crafts Council, and the Editors of Ceramic Review.

Above all, I am grateful to my wife Anne-Marie, who saw and shared almost all the contents of this book and helped it to take shape, but did not live to see it finished.

ACS

LOOKING FORWARD

1	PLACE	page	7
2	THE WORKSHOP	page	8
3	THROWING	page	12
4	WILLOWS	page	21
5	WOOD FIRING	page	27
6	PEOPLE	page	33
7	LUSTRE	page	44
8	SAID EL SADR	page	53
9	ASH TRAYS	page	61
10	GIPSY BOWLS	page	65
11	ART OR CRAFT	page	71
12	AN APPRENTICE	page	75
13	EXPORTS	page	81
14	BUSINESS	page	87
15	THE FACTORY	page	95
16	STATIONS OF THE CROSS	page	103
17	A PARTY	page	109
18	BIG POTS	page	114
19	SUNDIAL	page	123

LOOKING AROUND

20	CERAMICS	page	127
21	SKILL	page	133
22	CLAY	page	141
23	DECORATION	page	153
24	BORROWING	page	161
25	PATRONAGE	page	166
26	TIN	page	173
27	CREATION	page	179
28	WASTE	page	185
29	THE VISIT	page	189
30	CENTERING	page	199
31	ENVIRONMENT	page	205

LOOKING BACK

32	FINALE	page	209
	NOTES	page	212

POTTERY, PEOPLE AND TIME

Top: "...earthenware from the ground up, walls, roofs and chimneys."
Bottom: Bowl commemorating the 40th year of the Aldermaston and Wasing Produce Show, ACS, 1982.

I

PLACE

Aldermaston is best known today as the site of the atomic weapons establishment, whose perimeter begins at the top of the hill about a mile away. The village, however, existed well over a thousand years before and has a life of its own, far removed from the activities taking place nearby.

Most of the houses, including the Pottery building in the middle of the street, were built in the early eighteenth century of soft, reddish-pink brick from the clay that lies all around just under the soil. As some American potters once said, "You'd just have to work in earthenware here: the whole place is earthenware from the ground up, walls, roofs and chimneys."

A busy co-operative workshop has many facets, many of them unseen even by those who know the place well, and sometimes very unlike the P.R. image presented in art periodicals and press-releases. The pages that follow arise from some of the activities and exchanges going on behind the scenes.

The sequence reflects the way different aspects come to the fore, now one, now another – techniques, materials, people, projects, business, aesthetics – sometimes abruptly contrasting with one another, but all interconnected. Each in turn needs attention and the enterprise as a whole depends on the balance. Even so, as will be seen, the effects are not always predictable.

2

THE WORKSHOP

Dora Billington led me into pottery and ceramics through her much sought after evening classes at the Central School, for which I honour her memory and will always be grateful. Especially, I am grateful to her for explaining that what I wanted to do was tin-glaze earthenware. I had seen it in Spain but had never heard its name and had no knowledge of the technique, one which few other teachers at that time would have encouraged. She also winked at the college rules, allowing me to start earlier and earlier in the day, eventually as soon as the doors opened at 8.30 a.m. I had to make the best possible use of the time available; besides, I was captivated by the transformations, transformation of the formless into form, soft into hard, drabness into colour, and colour into movement and meaning. It was magical. I could hardly have kept away. I used to place my finished pots from the kiln on the floor by my bed so that I could touch them before sleeping and see them the moment I awoke. It was still difficult to believe how they had come alive by being fired in the kiln.

As a direct result of the thrill of working at the Central, trying to follow it up and if possible make a living from it, I started the Pottery in my home village. Finding a place to work in can often be a formidable problem, but in my case the solution fell into my lap: the disused smithy had been waiting for a new lease of life for several years. The problems came later and were of a different kind. I had to start on my own, but it was something I wanted to share and needed to share, because there was still so much to understand. Work is different when it is shared: the highs are more effervescent, the lows less daunting, and one learns new things in unexpected ways.

I had then, and have still, a feeling for pottery that is used. Pots of this kind are sometimes belittled by the label 'functional ware', as if they could have no interest beyond their potential use. Usefulness is in fact only one facet of their existence. The day-to-day work and the character of the finished pots themselves led me towards an open, collaborative workshop at a time when most of my contemporaries were establishing private studios. This was not evident at the time: ceramic transformations were so fascinating that the question of where I was going took second place.

Tin-glaze is unusual among ceramics, because as much time is spent decorating as in making the forms. Anyone working with assistants has to decide whether to follow the traditional custom of dividing up the work between specialised clay-workers and painters, or to involve everyone in both these aspects of the making. I was in no doubt. Unless everyone shared in both, they would miss the transformations and lose the heart of the matter.

It seemed best to spread the fun and the grind as evenly as possible. Sharing without specialising began as a practical need, but it continued as a principle. It is not the most productive system, but it provides an all-round training that enables people to stand on their own when the time comes. It needs patience; there is more to learn and everyone has to make more mistakes. No-one will ever equal the specialist skill of a traditional artisan, but something else comes instead: the chance to experience the transformations at every stage, and now and again to find something new emerging from the depths of the imagination and taking durable, tangible form. That is the most extraordinary transformation of all.

We had to establish a basic repertoire of painted forms and learn to repeat them. To do this, one has to see the differences between a row of almost identical pots, recognise which are the best, and begin to understand why. Above all, we had to devise forms that were good to decorate. Some forms need no decoration; others, like the classic albarello, are waiting for it. We also had to find the way to a 'language' of colour, pattern and movement and imagery that was not simply personal idiosyncrasy, but meant something to us all and carried conviction with those who came to buy. It needed to be distinct enough to be communicable, but also versatile and mysterious enough to hold the seeds of something new, to break its own boundaries. Only when this grounding had been established could we attempt to make anything genuinely different and special. That in its turn depended not only on our personal input, but on the materials, glazes and pigments. We needed to discover what they could do by means of a long series of trials and had gradually to learn how to coax out their qualities, especially during the glaze and lustre firings in the wood-fired kiln.

It took at least four people to build the first kiln while continuing to pay our way. By the time that kiln was demolished and replaced by a better one two years later, there

At the bench: David Tipler and Graham Adamson, 1972

were five of us. By the time we began to understand how to use it effectively, there were six, and before we understood much about reduction-lustre, we were eight.

The success of an enterprise depends on individuals as well as numbers. The indefinable corporate spirit changes every time a new person arrives. A collaborative workshop and its repertoire of ideas changes gradually and continuously from year to year. Certain projects, like the big lustre pots, are only possible for a particular group of people. With less than seven people, that project could never have been considered. It proved how valuable a close, self-reliant group of makers can be and we ourselves were all astonished to discover what could be done.

Over the years, many people contributed to the regular work of the Pottery and enriched it with new ideas and approaches. From amongst many, I think of Gwyn and the subtle, exacting clarity of her throwing; Edgar and his innate sense of the craftsmanlike way to do things; Laurence and the lyrical precision of his design and drawing; Jason's powerful forms and strangely convincing imagery; Julian's spirited way of rising to a challenge, especially his masterly throwing of the four-foot pots; Andrew's calm control of the lustre fire and the dancing rhythms of his brush. We all learned a great deal from each other, and my own work has been influenced by almost everyone I ever worked with. Yet all the variety and the frequent modifications of methods and materials have been unified by the discipline of the tin-glaze technique itself and by the potentialities residing within it, lit up by the transformations specially belonging to clay and fire.

People sometimes say that the workshop principle belongs to a past era and an obsolete philosophy of craftsmanship, and that it is socially and economically out of date. I don't believe it ever could be. In times of violence or instability, or in times of rapid inflation or recession, it becomes more difficult, as I learnt all too well later on. But collaborative work remains one of the most basic of all human relationships and though its structure may change it will always reappear when the sun comes out and it could never become obsolete.

3

THROWING

Originally I never thought of using the wheel. I was too busy making modelled figures. This was one of the many diversions from my studies at Cambridge. They were light-hearted and fairly crude and there was quite a vogue for them amongst my friends at King's. The clay came from a land-drain factory in the Newmarket road. When fired it came out a flesh-pink colour, which is why many of the figures were nudes, such as Cleopatra, Caligula coming out of the bath, and, at the request of Simon Raven, Arion returning to Corinth on a dolphin, and other male nudes. There were some clothed figures as well, especially poets and Irish labourers, and a number of animals. They were mostly around eight or nine inches high and were tucked into the kiln amongst the drain pipes.

As a result of this I got into conversation about clay with Julian Rea at a party. Julian had been taught to throw at Bryanston and was at that time giving adult education classes in the village college at Sawston. He insisted that I must try my hand at the wheel straight away. It was magic. The clay centred itself almost miraculously and before Julian could give me any instruction I had made a small bowl. He said this was not at all what was supposed to happen. People are expected to struggle and cry out for help. He put a white slip on the bowl and the next day I carved figures of animals through the slip with lino-cutting tools. He glazed it and a week later there in my room was my first finished pot, thick and slightly misshapen, but to my mind an object of remarkable beauty.

Whenever I could get to a wheel I practised on it and eventually acquired one of my own, but this first miracle never happened again. I made a considerable number of pots but they were all squat and lumpish and it was a battle all the way. Help was desperately needed but there was no-one to turn to. After struggling intermittently for two years I eventually got into evening classes at the Central School, where I was taught by Kenneth Clark and the stalwart Yorkshire potter Mr Bateson.

"Give yourself a chance!" he called out during our first class. "Don't forget to breathe." I thought they were going to show us holds and grips, but this unexpected advice was much more to the point. I was trying so hard that my breathing had almost stopped and my whole body was tense and unco-ordinated. No wonder the clay didn't spring to life as it had done that slightly intoxicated evening back at Sawston. Within a few weeks Mr. Bateson got me going again and in due course the lifts and grips followed, together with down to earth practical advice about types of clay and their consistency, the speed of the wheel, the amount of water, the use of tools and wires and ribbers, and above all one's physical position. "People think it's all done with the hands. That's a mistake. Real throwing starts there!" He tapped the lower part of my spine. Mr. Bateson retired many years ago but even now I seldom use the wheel without some of his advice coming vividly back to mind.

One thing they didn't teach at the Central was how to lift the soft, newly thrown pot off the wheel. Instead they had disks which were neatly pegged to the wheelhead and one simply lifted up the disk with the pot standing on it. When I started on my own I had no such disks and again and again the pots collapsed between my hands as I tried to lift them. To get to grips with this problem, I visited the flower-pot throwers at Tilehurst. They were using an extremely soft, sandy local clay and worked amazingly fluently. They drew up the clay, cupped it in their hands, and lifted pot after pot from the wheel hardly even looking at them. They couldn't explain, they just did it. I passed the whole afternoon with them, trying to figure it out. It looked so easy. The moment I got back home I took some soft clay and made a similar plant pot shape, imitating everything they had done as exactly as possible, the throwing, the cutting with the wire, the cupping the the hands and the rapid lift from the wheel to the board. Amazing sympathetic magic! The pot bowed slightly in my hands as I picked it up, but as soon as it was laid on the board it settled and became round again. Since that day lifting pots from the wheel has never been much of a problem. It is mainly a matter of timing and confidence.

I learnt something else from the flowerpot makers. They didn't explain, they just communicated the feel, and this is a most effective way of learning. Certain grips are unexpected and it helps to have them demonstrated, but throwing depends largely on confidence and getting the feel of the movement and this is most easily assimilated by imitation. Later, when I was trying to teach people myself, this experience turned out

POTTERY, PEOPLE AND TIME

Top: Normandy potter, about 1890.
Right: Throwers with tilted wheels: Fustat, Egypt, 1969.
Bottom: Thrown forms being beaten out: Nepal.

to be vitally important and it was usually possible to get people going in just the same way as the Tilehurst potters had helped me, through the movement and rhythm. As soon as the confidence comes, people begin to discover things for themselves. It applies to a great many other things too, such as brushwork, and to many other skills outside the field of pottery. Explanation and analysis are useful when things go wrong, but most people learn the essentials of throwing by imitation, the way a child learns to catch a ball.

Practice, unfortunately, does not always make perfect. During the next year I made a considerable number of pots and learnt to throw quite fluently. Periodically I would survey the clay population around me, initially with a certain satisfaction, but on looking more closely the imperfections became more and more evident. It was difficult to say quite what was wrong. They just looked slightly unborn. Then one day someone gave me a small Persian lustre bowl, damaged and considerably repaired, but still highly attractive. The little bowl felt so complete: the fine, deep foot rose to meet the curve of the underside with a beautiful precision; the rim flared slightly and delicately outwards to meet the surrounding space; it was a delight to run one's fingers across the clean curve of the inside, and above all, although it wasn't particularly thin, it felt light because it had a perfect balance in the hand. I realised then that I was leaving off where the real business of throwing begins. I was stopping with a simple basic form and not taking it far enough to become articulate. I needed to continue, sensing the curves and concavities better, seeing the proportions more clearly, and above all deciding what should happen at the rim. This was no longer a matter of manual skill. It was in the mind. I was working without seeing clearly enough what I was aiming at. My hands needed to be told what they were trying to do. Only then could the real throwing begin.

I tried drawing the shapes I had in mind on paper. This was helpful up to a point, but they didn't come alive. It hadn't any of the excitement that came from working direct with the clay. A better way was to make a quick, conceptual sketch and then determine the details when the clay was between one's hands. The sketch revealed the places where the important choices came and I could try out various alternatives. The best way was to make half a dozen versions of the same form. One of them would usually stand out as far better than the others. The next thing was to see what this depended on and then to try to do it again. That was easier said than done. It took ages to get anywhere near it. I was beginning to appreciate what throwing really involves. You do it with your hands but they have to be governed not only by the place low down in the spine but by the mind as well. These two kinds of sensibility have to come together. Left brain and right brain.

Then I discovered how important it was to have the right amount of clay. Once you know what you are trying to do you find that it could be done with far less clay than was originally used. The fact is, indecision requires a great deal of clay! Once you get into the throwing rhythm it can usually be done with three quarters of what you started with. From now on I kept a book of measurements recording the weights of clay needed for each shape of pot. This was a vital part of the work because it is just as difficult to throw well with too much clay as too little. When every ounce of clay is made to work properly the pot gets the feel of being slightly airborne, regardless of its actual weight.

The use that a pot was intended for turned out to be a vital part of throwing. It was a great help to remember that it had to be suitable for holding or pouring from, that it had to be easy to clean or to serve from with a spoon, or to hold flowers. All these things helped to determine the detailed features of the shape. Without these functional requirements the choices and articulations were apt to be merely a matter of arbitrary stylishness. They need not be: there are some magnificent vessels that have no specific use, but for a beginner it was helpful to accept the discipline imposed by a function. The whole idea was put in a beautiful nutshell by William Newland: "if you want to make a flower vase, first go and get some flowers". Function is in fact not a severe limitation: the variety of serviceable jug-shapes used in the cultures of the world is enormous, but all decent jugs fulfil the requirements of containing, holding, pouring, standing firm and cleaning and their features reflect these needs. Some of the meanest pots in the world are the ones made only for show, without any purpose.

The first time I watched throwers at work was in Triana, across the river from Seville. They were making small bowls and throwing 'off the hump', that is to say, centering a large cone of clay and making twenty or so small bowls by flaring out the top of the cone, shaping a bowl-form, and cutting it off with a thin cord. The beauty of this was that they were able to shape the entire piece and control the thickness very precisely right down to the foot and they could see everything clearly, including the underside, because it was up in front of them, not low down on the wheelhead. The pot was almost airborne and it always seemed to me desirable to make a pot as far as possible in the air, with the least possible attachment to the wheel. Throwing off the hump is done all over the world, wherever a large number of quickly made, small pots are wanted. Unfortunately, as I discovered, only certain clays are suitable for it. Some

THROWING

clays, like mine, tend to get an S-shaped split in the base of the pot as they dry because the lower part of the clay has not been compressed as much as the walls. The only way of avoiding this is to make forms with very small bases and some traditional pots have small bases for this very reason. For me, the technique proved ideal for making the stems of goblets. A couple of dozen stems could be made from one hump of clay, and the foot, the knop and the stem could be precisely shaped in full view almost up in the air, and the finished stem was finally severed from the hump with the flat blade of a paint-scraper.

I appreciated this technique all the more because much of my work at that time tended to be too solidly bottom-based. A form with a wide base is of course a safer proposition for the thrower. The clay can be drawn upwards and outwards, and in again if wished, without much risk of the lower part of the pot buckling or folding as it takes the pressure. The lower part is usually fined down when the clay is leather-hard by turning the pot upside down and trimming with a tool. None the less, turned or unturned, a great many European pots still retain their original bottom-heavy appearance. This has some advantages: a firmly-based pot sits steadily on a table, but some pots are too steady by half. Not even the wildest party can dislodge them, and many of our Western pots are distinctly lacking in lift, while Middle Eastern vessels almost always rise from relatively small bases with a gentle grace.

The explanation of this difference became clear the moment I watched potters working in Egypt. To make any kind of large, upright container vessel such as a jar or jug or waterpot, they worked in two stages. First they threw the basic form, finishing the whole of the shoulder, neck and rim precisely but leaving the lower wall quite thick. When the pot was severed from the wheel one saw that it had no base; the bottom was completely open. The pot was then left to dry slightly and stiffen in the warm air. The thin clay of the upper part naturally dried quicker than the rest, so that after about an hour the pot could be turned upside down and placed in a deep, thick ring of clay on the wheel. The softer clay of the thick, lower part was then thrown upwards, increasing the height of the pot, and finally inwards so that it actually joined, closing in the base. The base was now a smooth, convex curve. It could if wished be left as such, as is done with some of the traditional molasses jars and certain other vessels. Alternatively the potter could fashion a footed base by flattening the middle of the curved base and squeezing up a ring of clay around it to form a foot-ring. The pot was then taken away to dry. A handle was added, if required, once the lower part had become firm.

POTTERY, PEOPLE AND TIME

This process is what the Egyptian potters called 'turning', very different from the paring down with a tool which we call turning. Working as they did, no clay at all was trimmed away; every ounce of it was used and every part of the pot was directly worked by the hand. There was a beautiful economy about it and it explained why the forms of Islamic pots usually spring elegantly from the foot. I do not understand why the method is little known here. It is helped, of course, by the dry air of the Middle East, which stiffens the pots soon after they are made, and this is perhaps why it became normal practice there. In our part of the world one has to wait much longer before the vessels begin to dry, but the same effect can be achieved with the flame of a portable gas burner.

The day I watched this being done was only an introduction to the remarkable versatility of the traditional Islamic potter, which made our normal throwing techniques seem plodding and limited. Sometimes they would throw a tall neck or collar and put it to one side before making the pot for which it was intended. Then, when the pot was ready, they would place the soft collar in position and neatly attach it to the body of the pot as it spun on the wheel. Those tall-necked medieval Persian flasks and bottles must have been made in this way. Alternatively, they would add a soft ring of clay to the inturning shoulder of a vessel and draw it up into a collar, with no risk of running short of clay for the rim, as often happens when a pot is made from a single ball. In a similar manner they would fashion a deep foot under a bowl, either from a ready-thrown ring of clay or an applied coil, and in both cases the foot would be directly shaped by hand rather than trimmed with a tool. The highly articulated forms of Islamic pots derive naturally from this versatile way of working, which traditional potters perform wonderfully swiftly. It involves specific skills that potters elsewhere do not usually acquire, but anyone who can throw reasonably well could learn them fairly easily. When I first saw it being done I felt, once again, that I was just beginning to recognise what real throwing is about.

Another variety of throwing is the expansion of a form by beating. I don't think this is done in the Middle East but it is well known in India and Nepal. A form such as a round jar is allowed to stiffen slightly and is then expanded by beating the wall with an implement such as a rounded stone from the inside and by a light wooden paddle on the exterior. Again, the clay is thrown sufficiently thick to allow for the expansion that the potter forsees when the beating is done. This method is capable of producing subtle forms whose profiles are slightly softened from the original thrown vessel, and which can if wished be deliberately beaten out of the round. The gradual process of beating also enables the potters to determine the profile very sensitively as they proceed.

I have not seen the beating process, but I have watched a related and perhaps even more ancient method of making bowls being done by jungle potters in Sri Lanka. They did not even have a wheel. The women threw a ring from a ball of clay resting on a flattish, round piece of stone which they rotated on a rock. The ring of clay was thick at the base and thinner at the rim. Once it had half dried it was taken to another potter, an immensely fat man who evidently seldom moved. He sat on a kind of bamboo throne and had beside him a rounded piece of wood something like a shoe-maker's last. Placing the leather hard ring of clay against the wood, he beat it with a small wooden paddle, turning it round all the time, making the thick clay spread inwards to meet in the middle, forming a closed, convex base. These simple terracotta bowls were fired in a clamp of coconut husks. They are used in all the villages for cooking over charcoal and are sold for next to nothing. Pots are made in a similar way in many parts of Africa and this method has probably been used since the Stone Age. The forms are often subtle and beautiful and would not look out of place in the Design Centre.

Centering my first bowl at Cambridge, I could never have guessed how much I would learn about throwing in the following years. Whatever one may learn, it is only a fraction of all that is known. There is no single right way of throwing. The principles are the same everywhere but it is done differently all over the world. Greek potters normally throw with the wheel at their side, not in front of them. The Arabs traditionally use a wheel tilted away from the thrower, with a shaft pivoting on the knee-bone of a camel. Few of us could manage to work in the squatting position that is customary in India. The wheel is rotated with a stick, since it must not be touched by the foot in deference to Shiva, while most western potters prefer a motorised wheel with a variable resistance speed-control unit. Yet good pots are made in all these different circumstances and everyone has to discover how to make the best use of whatever is available.

Throwing is of course only one way of making pots; there are many other good ways and each has some particular virtue. Throwing, however, seems to me now even more remarkable than it did in the beginning. How strange that in many colleges of art it is looked down upon as insensitive and mechanical.

One of the special features of throwing is its immediacy. I once asked Jason Shackleton, who was working with me, whether he would like to try his hand at coiling a large pot we had been asked for. "Not me!" He looked dismayed. "I'm an instant potter. I like quick results". But of course before anyone can enjoy quick results there is a great deal to learn. Not everyone wants to spend the necessary time on it. Some people get disheartened and give it up. Others, including many amateur potters, prefer various kinds of hand-building that do not demand the same mobile discipline. Some teachers are suspicious of throwing on the grounds that it can become slick and unfeeling and their doubts are justified. A production thrower working with a good clay can produce instant results all too easily; bland, anonymous pots, whipped unthinkingly off the wheelhead, thrown without any clear concept. This is a kind of blasphemy against the real thing. The quality of a thrown pot sometimes depends on the clay not being too good. A lean clay forces the potter to pay attention; he has to be clear what he is aiming at and he cannot take liberties. Part of the magic of throwing is the interplay of dominating the material and yielding to it. The strong pressure that is needed in one part of the form leads elsewhere into a gentle caress. The same balance occurs in sailing a boat and many sailors are also good throwers, and vice-versa. For both of them, timing is vital. As the clay spins on the wheel, the thrower initiates the lift and the expansion of the form. Then suddenly he finds himself following the clay rather than forming it. It feels as if it is rising by itself, and all he has to do is to keep in time.

"Keep time with the clay and the magic begins," Michael Cardew used to say. "Then you discover what Omar Khayyam meant when he asked which is the potter, pray, and which the pot? It's not a rhetorical question: he knew exactly what he was talking about."

4

WILLOWS

It has been the most exquisite autumn day and we have been working out of doors almost until sunset. Not simply out of doors, but beside the silvery waters of the Kennet. Where I was today the river is flanked by willows, poplars and alders and their leaves are just turning colour and come fluttering down in the sunlight into the wide fields on either side like flakes of gold. To be in such a place at all is good, but to be able to take it in gently and little by little, by being a working part of it, that's best of all.

Andrew and I took the Landrover and trailer to where the foresters had felled some willows the week before. We spent the day sawing logs and splitting them ready for stacking in the wood-yard behind the Pottery, where they will dry for a year before being used for firing the big kiln. They dry best out in the open, exposed to sun, wind and frost, and in time they lose nearly half their weight as the moisture is drawn out of them.

We collect wood at various times all through the year, but most often in late summer and early autumn, when the terrain is driest and most accessible.

There's naturally a good deal of feeling against felling trees. Everyone misses their towering forms and people are apt to protest that the land is being denuded and the earth's atmosphere is becoming more polluted than ever. These willows are a special case, however. They are grown all along the Kennet valley as a crop, a crop with a cycle of some thirty years, and they are 'harvested' for cricket-bats, which are eventually exported throughout the Commonwealth. It's a flourishing business, and new trees are staked out every year, usually in late February, more than making up for those that have been cut down. Near the spot where we were working, young trees five, ten, fifteen years old were growing along the river and beside the dykes between the fields, spaced at intervals of about twenty feet. Amongst the vast variety of willows the bat-willow is easily recognised by the upward thrust of the branches and the silvery colour of the leaves.

New trees are propagated by cutting a 'stock' or pole of green wood from the top of a tree that has just been felled. The stock, about nine feet long, is trimmed and about a third of its length is thrust into the ground. New shoots begin to develop almost immediately and within three years it looks like an immense brush, with wands six or eight feet long sticking out on all sides. These are cut off and planted about two feet deep in moist ground. They set roots and begin to grow very rapidly. Periodically the trunk is trimmmed up to a height of about fifteen feet to keep the wood straight and free of knots while the tree grows, remarkably quickly, to a gracious, flame-like shape about forty or fifty feet high, and then its turn has come to be felled. The best willows are 'the greenest wood from the greenest wood' because the quickest growth makes the straightest and most springy material for cricket-bats.

Only the best wood from the trunk is used for bats. Any piece with a knot or a twist or an internal stain, and all the branch-wood, is useless,– useless even for logs in domestic fires because it spits furiously as it burns and anyway it burns away extremely fast. The reject wood is usually piled into a bonfire near where the tree fell, in order to clear the field for the farmer. When we need wood, however, the foresters leave all the larger pieces for us to collect for the kiln.

They saw the best wood into twenty-eight inch lengths (the size of a bat) and later split each section into clefts. The clefts are stacked to dry and are eventually trimmed down to a set size on the circular saw. So we take not only some of the trunk-wood and the branches but also the trimmings of the good clefts, and all that locked-in heat is used for hardening the clay, melting glazes and making colours. It pleases me that so much can be done with waste material. A year from now the green bark of the poles we got to-day will have turned golden and it will burst into flames in the furnace the moment it leaves your hand.

I've collected willow in all kinds of weather, half naked in the hottest summer, in the balm of harvest-time, carefully, because wasps have a passion for the sweet sap of the willow and cluster on the new wood, and in winter wind and frost too. All the seasons are good, but the bright autumn days are best of all.

From time to time we rested to cool down, wondering at the light playing over the tawny fuzz of dried field grass, the meadows on the far bank receding to a sequence of hedges, thickets, copses, distant fields and misty woods and finally the soft shadowy

WILLOWS

Top: Young willow, an ever-graceful tree.
Bottom: Splitting willow logs. Andrew Hazelden and ACS, 1992

blue of the hills. A pair of swans glided down-river; water-hens, coot and mallard were feeding and now and again disputing with loud squawks and splashing, and from time to time one caught sight of the dark back of a trout idling rhythmically against the current. You can't take it all in at once, but by working in it you absorb it gradually, becoming part of it through your eyes, lungs and limbs and something of it remains within you for ever. It also brings a special kind of companionship. We get a great deal done without any strain; Andrew always seems to be in the right place with the right implement at the right moment. We speak very little but sense each other's presence all the better for the silence, broken only by the stroke of the axe, the hammer striking the wedge and the shearing sound of the split wood.

How lucky we are that these willows fire our pots so well. It's not just a fuel but an exceptionally good one, especially for earthenware. The thermal value of the wood is low, but it releases its heat quickly and burns with a very long, soft flame, making a kiln atmosphere that gives a pearly whiteness to the glazes and a luminous depth to most of the colours. Four centuries ago Piccolpasso wrote in the *Three Books* that it is the best of all fuels for maiolica, and here as in many other matters he was absolutely right.

An old friend of ours, who was a management consultant for most of his working life, asked me once if wood-firing is really economic and not just a sentimental luxury, giving the illusion of real work while actually being a waste of time and energy. So far as I can estimate the costs, it compares favourably with electricity, for which the local cables would be inadequate anyway, and breaks about level with gas, even allowing for the cost of our time. But it produces better results than either and it also has a positive effect on everyone's morale. Everyone has something in each wood-firing and everyone takes their turn in fuelling it, and this is a cohesive, unifying factor for each member of the workshop, very different from turning on switches or adjusting gas-pressure. It can of course be tiring, but you must set beside that the experience of the transformation of material that is one of the basic appeals of ceramics, and, unless the firing is very poor, this gives back more energy than it takes.

Our good friend, who helped me a great deal in many ways, went on to say that anyway the boss should not go wood-gathering; he is forfeiting his responsibility as manager, designer, paymaster and so forth. Perhaps he was right, though I knew he was half teasing, so I replied that he will perform these responsibilies all the better for a few days out in the open. Anyone who can't allow himself that amount of time really is managing things badly. After all, he should be allowed the occasional holiday, where no-one can telephone or ask awkward questions or remind him of things left undone.

And what better holiday than such a day as this? A holiday isn't simply a day doing nothing. Isn't one of the meanings of the word 'holiday' the enjoyment of the wholeness of things, the way all things are linked together and ourselves with them?

Our old friend really knew this very well for he loved woodlands himself and had planted many trees. "Well, my dear Alan", he answered, schoolmaster-fashion, "you may despise the concept of maximum profit – though most professional men would not – but do not neglect the small matter of adequate profit, or your holidays, in every sense of the word, will rapidly come to an end!"

The sun was almost down as the Landrover humped its load back to the woodyard. A few drousy wasps were hovering over the sugary sapwood of the newly split branches. We unloaded with care in the fading light.

The end of the firing: view through the embers to the passages under the kiln chamber.

5

WOOD FIRING

Only around ten potters in the British Isles still fire with wood. Large industrial kilns are computer-controlled and fired with electricity, oil or gas, for obvious reasons (though Sèvres porcelain is still wood-fired), while most studio potters work singly and need small kilns fired with the minimum of labour. In any case, wood-fired kilns smaller than about fifty cubic feet in capacity are seldom satisfactory. When we first considered the possibility of using wood we had four people's work to fire, including some quite large items, and wood-firing seemed to make good sense. Alternative fuels were gas or oil, but since reject wood from cricket-bat willows was locally available it was the most attractive option. In the long run the benefits were far greater than we ever expected. Woodfiring extended the range of what we could make and it gave the glazes and colours a subtlety and completeness beyond anything we had done before.

Pine and fir are the timbers usually preferred. They do very well for stoneware and porcelain, but earthenware glazes with any lead content are easily blistered by the reduction (shortage of oxygen in the kiln atmosphere), which is difficult to avoid with resinous wood. For earthenware, clean, light woods such as willow and poplar are better, and were mentioned long ago by Cipriano Piccolpasso in his *Three Books of the Potter's Art*, written in 1557. Even so, the glazes can be spoiled by fly-ash and reduction can still occur, and in traditional kilns the ware is packed in saggars (fire-clay boxes) for protection. Inevitably the saggars take up much of the space and increase the cost.

In our first wood-fired kiln saggars were used in the belief that they were essential. It was a down-draught kiln with a self-supporting catenary arch, a fire-box at each end to equalise the spread of the heat, and a large chimney to produce sufficient upward pull. Unfortunately the two fireboxes simply doubled the labour of firing it, the down-draught caused too much reduction, and the catenary arch brought about a turbulent air-flow that scattered ash everywhere. Ray Finch, who fired with wood a generation before me, was proved absolutely right when he warned me, at the beginning "Your first kiln won't work well, but it will teach you a lot. Be prepared to take it down and build something better."

The design of the second kiln took these lessons into account. It has a long passage for the flames through the fire-box, so that reduction can be controlled by opening inlets for additional air. The interior differs from traditional up-draught and down-draught kilns. Instead, the draught of flame moves almost in a circle, entering under the floor of the chamber, rising up the rear wall. turning back under the semi-circular vault and curling down again under another part of the floor before being pulled up the chimney. The flow of the flames is so smooth that saggars are not needed, since no ash falls on the exposed pots.

Not all glazes respond to wood-firing. Some glazes containing calcium carbonate (usually from dolomite or whiting) may blister and do better in fully oxidising conditions but most of our own glazes are improved by wood-firing. I was surprised to discover (since I have never seen it mentioned in any book) that a certain amount of reduction is beneficial. Short spasms of reduction, up to about half a minute, alternating with periods of two or three minutes of clear burning, definitely improve the glazes and enrich most of the painted colours.

The wood is dried for a year in the open. Wind and sun and frost pull out the moisture. Damp wood gives far less heat and prolongs the firing. The firebox has three stoke-holes, which are refilled in turn every two or three minutes as the full temperature of 1060°C. is approached. This limits reduction and keeps the firebox at an even heat. If the wind is gusty, the fanning out of the flames passing through the interior of the kiln is controlled by slightly opening or closing secondary air inlets at each side of the firebox. The speed of the draught is controlled by dampers on each side of the chimney.

Packing the kiln, the firing itself and the subsequent emptying and sorting usually takes about five days. It cannot be done in a hurry; a thousand or more pots are in it and one firing can represent over ten per cent of a year's turnover. The packing requires two people, one positioning the pots on shelves inside the chamber and one passing them in, together with the necessary shelves, supports, cranks, baffles and stilts, and sometimes candles, matches and mirrors, to make sure that none of the surfaces are touching each other at the back. There is an ideal place somewhere for every shape, glaze and colour, if only it can be found. All the tables and benches nearby are covered with boards full of pots so that everything is clearly visible and it is easier to find the right piece. At this stage one can scarcely believe that so many things could ever be fitted in. The internal arrangement is planned in relation to the largest pots, for which only a few positions are suitable. One large vessel may occupy as much space as sixty smaller items, but it represents vastly more work and if it fires well it should have a far higher value.

Beginning at the back of the chamber, rows of heavy shelves, one inch thick, are set in position on vertical props and gradually loaded with pots until they rise stage by stage to within about eight inches of the curve of the vault. The space above is left free for the passage of the flames. A gap of about two inches is left between the shelves at each end and those in the middle to allow flames and ventilation to pass between them, aerating the glazes. Gradually the kiln packer works backwards through the chamber towards the entry door, always keeping the upper range of pots as level as possible so that the draught passes evenly under the vault all the way along. It is slow, careful work and at times there seems to be no progress, only cramped legs and an aching spine, but little by little the racks of pots on the tables thin out and by the time the packer reaches the near end of the kiln he usually has to get extra things painted to occupy the remaining spaces.

On the shelves nearest the doorway pyrometric cones are placed so as to be visible through spyholes in the kiln door. The cones are made of materials that melt at intervals of twenty degrees centigrade and they are the most reliable indicators of temperature. The kiln is also equipped with two thermocouple pyrometers, which are useful indicators of the rise or fall of the heat during the firing, but in my experience they seldom agree with the cones.

When eventually the chamber is full, all that remains is to build up the door, which consists of about a hundred numbered lightweight firebricks, topped by curved bricks fitting the arch over the entrance. The area around the kiln is swept clean and everything is ready for the firing to begin in the dark at four o' clock the next morning.

It starts slowly, with only a few pieces of light wood in the front of the firebox, to avoid the risk of cracking a large pot with sudden heat. The temperature rises throughout the day at about 70°C. an hour and the person minding the fire records it on a graph alongside the programme that has been drawn out. The fire becomes easier to manage as it gets bigger and it becomes steadily hungrier for wood as the day passes. Wisps of smoke begin to issue from between the bricks around the firebox, each new log crackles instantly as it slides into the flames and the whole area is filled with the familiar honeyish fragrance of burning willow bark. Everything is coming alive.

All three stoke-holes are in use by about 450°C. and fuel is added more and more frequently as the day goes on until eventually each position is recharged with several logs about every four minutes. The door to the stoke-hole nearest the kiln is left slightly ajar to allow extra air into the flow of the flame so that the combustion is carried right into the kiln chamber. Once the glazes begin to melt they shine. They are observed every ten minutes or so through the upper spy-hole to make sure that they are smooth. By this time the pots are shimmering with whitish-yellow heat and their forms can be clearly seen through the fingers of flame, against the slightly softer glow of the kiln walls. Any blisters that may have developed through lack of oxygen will be clearly seen on the clear line of a pot's rim or profile. If any unevenness is noticed, the fire has to be slackened, allowing more air in, and gradually the blisters will subside and smooth over. This prolongs the firing but it saves hundreds of pounds worth of pots.

After about twelve hours the kiln radiates a good deal of heat and those who are stoking the fire at this phase are apt to become hot and tired and it can seem as if the firing will never end. At a certain point it seems that the temperature in the kiln will not increase however much fuel one throws on the fire. Is the draught strong enough? Is the wood really dry? Are the logs too thick? Are the pyrometers working properly? Has something collapsed?

In fact it is only fatigue and everything is really quite all right. A little while later, by early evening, the first of the upper four cones begins to bend, which means that we are within about 60°C. of the full temperature. By this time the outer walls of the kiln are too hot to touch and the air over the rounded top of the firebox shimmers like a mirage. In winter, darkness is setting in by this time and the glare of the heat through the spyholes seems to have extra intensity. Each time the fire is refuelled a tongue of orange flame shoots out from a gap beside the upper spyhole. This is caused by unburnt gas suddenly igniting as it meets the air. It lasts for about fifteen seconds and then dies down as the first flush of combustion slackens and clear burning follows. However often you have fired the kiln before, you can't help being amazed that logs of wood could generate such a dense mass of heat, held in by tons of glowing bricks, with the pots standing out blinding yellow-white in the midst of it. The nearest of them are within arm's reach, yet they are in another world. We all have something in there and we are all feeling the same. The firing unites us. The physical proximity of so much brilliant heat is awesome. The beauty and wonder of it bring new energy.

New logs are slid across the hobs into the fire every two minutes and the temperature rises steadily, but more slowly as time goes on because of the heat being lost by the brickwork. During the next forty minutes the second and third cones bend, lean over and go down. Only the last cone remains. In the dazzling heat it is sometimes difficult to see. If necessary, you blow at it through a tube and the cool air makes it visible for a few seconds. When this cone goes half down the full temperature will have been reached. Once it begins to lean a little, the dampers in the chimney are pushed slightly further in, restricting the draught and pressing heat back into the corners of the chamber. Now the fire is stoked less heavily, avoiding any reduction and holding the heat steady. During the next fifteen minutes the cone slowly softens until it is almost down, a peaceful end to the final act. The kiln is sealed and left to cool for two days.

One does not take risks with a big firing: ten per cent of the turnover is still ten per cent whether you're Wedgwood's or a family business. Firings are meant to be as consistent as possible, but in practice no two are quite the same. The internal arrangement always varies according to the dimensions of the largest pots. Weather sometimes has a considerable influence too and other explicable and inexplicable variables give each firing its own unique character. There have been a few bad firings over the years, but the memory fades beside those that have been good or exhilarating. A potter taking his work from the kiln is seeing and touching an object that the fire has transformed into something completely new. It may come out as he expected, but in a really good firing the pots emerge with characteristics that no-one could ever have exactly foreseen. Unpacking a wood-firing has a feeling of exploration about it, however often it is done.

Emptying the kiln, sorting the pots, putting the orders aside and carrying everything indoors takes four people the best part of a day, by the end of which time every table and shelf and cupboard in the building seems to be overflowing with pots, shining with light and colour, and much of the floor space too. One wanders amongst it slightly dazed, discovering, comparing, learning lessons for the future, but principally simply enjoying the mass of the things that have been transformed by the trial of the fire. The amount the kiln holds is always a surprise. The whole sequence of events takes long enough that by the time it is over, one no longer remembers what went in at the beginning.

Wood-firing is sometimes said to be uneconomic and motivated mainly by romantic idealism. Certainly it has a romantic aspect, but it is done because it makes technical and human sense in a particular context: few if any other kinds of firing bring such sensitive contact with the sequence of transformations that underlies all work with clay, glaze and colour.

6

PEOPLE

Our visitor had been quietly looking around on his own for some time, but I was very much aware of his presence and although he hadn't spoken we knew he was enjoying himself. He was a man of about my age, in casual, stylish clothes, and he took an interest in a number of things that most people never notice. Catching my eye and speaking with the springy drawl of the Southern States, he pointed to a rusty old epèe that I bought years ago in Newbury and which hangs on the ring that Bert Cox used for tying up the feet of restless horses.

'Mr. Smith', he called out, 'will you tell me Sir, could that sword be from the Civil War time?'

He was evidently no fencing man, but his history was correct. This part of England saw a good deal of action during the Civil War. There were battles at Newbury in 1641 and 1644 and several cavalry skirmishes around Aldermaston itself, and some of the dead are buried up at Rag Hill a mile away.

He must have been wondering whether the Pottery had existed ever since those days, as could easily be supposed from the old building with its weathered brickwork, in a street which can't have looked very different when the cavalry cantered through it. I was tempted to weave a romantic story around my 'sword' and at that moment I was half sorry that my helpers were not descended from families of artisans who plied their trade all through the wars and plagues and insurrections of long ago.

I've had the same feeling myself when visiting old workshops on the continent, the sense that man and material have been matched in a certain place from time immemorial. It helps us to believe that the past really existed and it gives us a sense of belonging. Nonetheless, I had to disappoint our visitor with the truth.

'Still," he said, "this surely is the way things would have been?'

Top: Nic Werner, Andrew Hazelden and Mohamed Hamid, 1984.
Bottom: Decorating: Edgar Campden and Julian Bellmont, 1991.

PEOPLE

Looking at Edgar's bearded profile as he bent over his work, and Mike with his lean, purposeful features, I could well imagine them in the working-garb of long ago. As for Jason, with his assured bearing and curling, auburn hair, he behaves all the time like Cavalier portrait come to life, while Laurence looks every inch a steadfast captain on the side of the Parliament. The human head intent on a job of work is timeless and it's not difficult to transpose a familiar face back across the ages.

'It wouldn't have been much different.'

Very likely. After all, for centuries the most practical way of making many things was through a small group of self-reliant people, fashioning material with simple equipment, passing on their skills one to another and trading from their place of work. It was pre-industrial, not in the sense that there were no machines, for there were – looms, lathes, pumps, furnaces and potters' wheels are all machines – but in that the things made depended more on human skill than on capital and machinery and on shared understanding rather than on a programmed system. Many things are still done in this way not only in the Third World but in the affluent West, from jewellery and dressmaking to boat-building and hot air balloons.

Traditional potteries operate through a division of labour. The pattern has held good for centuries and a similar kind of specialisation is an essential feature of the industrial system. It makes economic sense but it isn't entirely satisfying on a human level. Specialisation requires a lot of repetitive work, and not too much initiative. A well-known potter once dismissed one of his apprentices with the comment, "She was no use to me. She had ideas". He wasn't being fair. Repetition and consistency are essential in any skill, but it's not unreasonable to look for something more. Today some different, more co-operative pattern is called for in a working team, something that allows for innovation and 'seizing the moment' in addition to the steady work that sees things through.

This is why instead of dividing up the activities into specialised branches, I tried to do the opposite, gradually introducing each person to every process. The idea is that everyone should eventually be able to do every part of the work and understand it. Since each process depends on the others, it's good to take part in them all and be as closely as possible aware of how everything fits together . It can't happen overnight. To get it all well and truly together might take a life-time, but the nearer it comes, the better for everyone.

The American looked doubtful as I tried to explain this. It might be good for people, he said, but how good was it for business? Wasn't there a conflict of interests?

There certainly is. In small ways it crops up every day. In the short term, trying to teach everything to everyone, instead of establishing specialised roles, looks like a waste of time and energy. Some commercial opportunities are missed, admittedly, but in the long run it makes sense. A business based on creative work depends on each individual's quality and enthusiasm, and people only put their heart into it if they understand the work and enjoy each other's company. Differences of temperament and background inevitably lead to occasional frictions, but these are minor matters compared with the values that draw people together.

He saw immediately that a lot depends on finding the right kind of people and asked whether I looked for them or whether they applied to me.

I said that it works both ways. The connection usually comes about by hearsay or personal contact, which are natural screening processes. Not everyone would fit. Loners wouldn't like it; egocentrics would exploit the system and even if they are excellent potters it's best to avoid them. Nor, as a rule, would I take on people with no previous training. There is an informal agreement that people come for not less than two years. As time goes on they become more productive and the second year usually balances out the introductory period. Most people stay far longer, but eventually they leave, usually to set up on their own. Then someone else fills their place and the process starts all over again. It's informal, but it works.

He nodded and surprised me by asking, "Meantime, what's the mortar that holds the bricks together?'

He explained that he was in the building business. Apparently the principal difference between various kinds of mortar is the proportion of cement and lime in the mix. There are hard mortars and soft ones, which he called 'giving mortar'. Each kind has its particular uses. He said that in most businesses it's the hard mortar that counts, meaning money, influence, status and so forth . For them, he said, people can be persuaded to do almost anything, good or bad. And then comes fear, fear of the future, fear of missing out, which he regarded as the hardest mortar of all. But he said that sometimes a soft mortar works better; it gives and holds when the hard kind would break the fabric.

I liked the point he was making and was enjoying his company and it was rather pleasing to be asked if I could spare the time to show him more of the workshop.

Jason was at the big wheel, half way through making a large, tall jar, and next to him Gill was wiring off one of a series of small bowls. Beside her stood a pyramid of weighed-out lumps of clay. Jason had reached the tricky moment when the shoulder of the jar has to be turned inwards to gather in a broad ring at the top. The soft form trembled on the verge of deforming and there was silence except for the whirr of the wheel. He eased the clay gently inwards, raising and lowering his head as if coaxing it into place, as he always did when he was concentrating. If the clay is too wet or too thin the shoulder will droop when pressure is applied and sometimes the pot simply folds up on itself. I held my breath. Jason brought the shape inwards and consolidated the rim with a deft touch, trimmed the foot with the V-ended tool, wired off the base and lifted the pot on to a board. It was a good moment to be watching. His ear-ring glinted as he flicked his head and he looked debonair as ever, but there was sweat on his brow. He drew a deep breath and smiled.

"Like to try your hand?" he asked, pleased with the way things had gone. "But you're not dressed right for the job, are you? Another time, perhaps. By the way, these pots are going to be lamps for the library of an antiquarian book-dealer. A very elegant place. Eventually they'll be painted in red and silver lustre."

"Will you be doing that?"

"I'll be painting them, following Alan's prototype, but we've got to dry them and glaze them first and the lustre firing's months away yet. We only have four a year. If you come back at Christmas you'll be able to judge for yourself how they come out."

Some people are natural big throwers and Jason is at his best on a large scale. His work has a natural, flowing feeling, in tune with his make-up. It has flair, and though he can throw and paint very delicately when he wishes, he is one of those people who can work for hours on the wheel with hardly any strain. He broke off the conversation to turn to Gill, beside him, who was obviously in difficulties.

"Don't watch me," she said, slightly embarrassed. "I'm learning these. They're meant to be swallow bowls and they're coming out all shapes and sizes. It's maddening. They're really so simple."

Jason was showing her how to lift the side, keeping the base small and trim. Everyone learns all over again by teaching, because you can only pass on what you yourself understand. Giving or accepting help is more than a technical matter. Learning goes by jumps; a person sometimes struggles for ages without seeming to improve, then suddenly everything comes together. It's exhilarating and to see it happen to your own pupil is the best of all. In due course the one who is learning will pass it on to someone else. It creates a bond between people. Perhaps it's one aspect of the soft mortar.

"She's new to these," explained Jason, "but she's doing very well considering. You see, she only had an art school training."

Gill made a face. It was a recurrent tease. Potters like Jason and me, who never had much of a formal training, tend to look down on people who have been systematically taught but haven't yet adjusted to the momentum of a practical workshop that has to pay its way. An art school training can give a wide spread of knowledge and ideas but it seldom teaches people how to use time economically, or how to sustain the effort. Gill is in fact a natural 'small thrower', neat handed, thoughtful and imaginative. Once she understands a design she develops it stage by stage, always with an unmistakable, original touch.

Our visitor asked if she also did decoration.

"That's the idea. Actually I've decorated some of the bowls already, but when you come back to making a shape the second or third time round it gets easier because you know what makes it paintable. If the shape's right the painting is so easy. Anyway, my first attempts have all gone. They were marked at half-price and they sell easily. The smaller things always do."

"On the other hand," interposed Jason, "if these lustre jars come out well they'll cost a lot. They're not easy, and the lustre firing is always a risk. But they're fun all the same."

People who work here could only be content with a 'giving mortar'. Most of them have too much initiative to be happy under a rigid system and fortunately most of them stay far longer than the period of our initial agreement. I think this is partly because the scope of the work is open-ended; new projects can arise at any moment; there is always something more to learn and something new to contribute. The business has in fact proved more stable than most. Don Zver once flew over from Canada armed with a tape-recorder and clip-board to discover what he called the 'Aldermaston System' and apply it to his own studio. He went back little the wiser, though his tape included several clear chimes from my grandfather clock. "The trouble is", he said later, "it's as much an atmosphere as a system and you can't get it down on paper."

Crossing the yard to the rear workshop we were halted for a moment by a melodious voice at full volume singing "Much too much in love to say good-night". It was Mike thumping wads of rough clay into the pug-mill, which extruded them in long, even rolls, ready for use. His arms and apron were splattered with clay-slops, but the fruits of his effort lay in a neat stack almost filling the further bench.

"Not my favourite job", he said, wiping his brow with the back of his hand. "Want to take over?"

"I'll pass."

"That's how we all feel. We take turns. There's the rota on the wall, and my turn doesn't come round again for another four weeks. Tomorrow I'll get back to decorating."

"You enjoy that?"

"I used to hate it. I'm really a clay man. I'd done no decorating at all till I came here, and it was a struggle all the way. But it grows on you. Most of our shapes are meant for decoration and the pots wouldn't be right without it. Besides, it makes a nice change."

The variety of the work is important, even though certain jobs are nobody's favourite. The closer everything comes together the better each activity makes sense. The specialised roles of traditional manufacture in the past must often have been desperately monotonous, whereas a co-operative workshop involves the different sides of each person. Some of the work is physically energetic, like Mike's present job and Jason's work at the wheel, while decorating is relatively peaceful. Some jobs are repetitive; others depend on imagination and taking leaps in the dark. The formulation of glazes and colours is systematic and technical, while commissions involve dealing with people, agreeing prices, interpreting ideas and sometimes persuading. Each kind of work depends on the others and everyone knows it.

Mike slung more clay into the mill, bringing the long lever down to press it into the extruding-chamber.

"You see you have to press down slowly. If you go too fast it puts air bubbles into the clay and then it's useless. The timing has to be right. So does the consistency. Too hard or too soft is a waste of effort. It may not seem so, but there's quite an art to this job. Are you sure you don't want to take over? Yes, I know, the next room's far more interesting. Nice to meet you."

The silence in the rear workshop was a contrast. Through a cloud of tobacco smoke I introduced our visitor to Edgar, who was painting a series of eleven-inch bowls with a delicate leaf-design, one that he has perfected over the years. Acknowledging us, he resumed his brushwork. We watched in silence. It is always absorbing to see a design take shape, arriving as if from nowhere, though of course it already exists in the painter's mind. Edgar seldom goes out of his way to make contact with visitors. He is a natural and all-round craftsman. He works almost as well in metal, glass, leather or wood as in clay, and his workshop at home is a den of well-worn and lovingly maintained tools and machinery. Our visitor could see that one does not disturb Edgar in the middle of a job. I was surprised when Edgar himself broke the silence.

He said that the bowls he was painting were one of the items most in demand, and also one of the most profitable, so it was important to ensure that we always had them in stock, but if any of them fired specially well they might be reserved for an exhibition. We had a dozen or so regular bowl designs but this was one of his favourites.

New designs are introduced every year but minor changes are being made all the time. Simply by repeating them you become aware of improvements or variations, and few designs stay exactly the same for long. It's quite different from a factory, and most people who deal with us understand that and appreciate it. Keeping the designs down to manageable numbers is the main problem.

"The hardest job is how to eliminate things," Edgar added. "Alan and I usually bring out the firing squad when we start again after New Year. It's hellish, but it has to be done."

The Pottery has to be firm enough to show what it stands for and vital enough to change or eliminate designs without losing its roots. The design ideas need to be generous, so that each person can assimilate them in their own way, but there are times when some particular feature has to be worked for very hard, analysing faults and trying again and again until it comes right. It is more than a studio version of quality-control. It's an exercise in seeing clearly. Criticism is often uncomfortable for everyone but it is a vital meeting-point.

Edgar re-lit his pipe, turned the next bowl upside down and painted a sign inside the foot-ring.

"My mark", he explained. "Everyone has their own. A for Aldermaston combined with the letter of their name. You can see them on the card up in the showroom."

"Isn't that confusing? Most manufacturers have only one."

"We've always done it this way," Edgar commented. "It's better all round, for lots of reasons, if you think about it."

He started the next bowl. The conversation was clearly over.

Further back, Laurence was working on a wide bowl with an extensive inscription and a large frog looking at a pool in the centre. You could feel the concentration, and it showed in his bearded face as he leant over his brush. He has a thoughtful disposition but is often less serious than he seems. When he looked up I introduced our visitor.

"That's beautiful, delicate work. But why the frog?"

"It's commissioned by one of the schools in the area. Eton, I think. It's a leaving present for a French master."

"A red frog strikes me as rather unusual."

"I believe he has left wing tendencies." Laurence paused. "But there's more to it, as you'll appreciate if you know the Hindu scriptures. It says somewhere that man is like a frog burning to death in the sand, but with three jumps he could liberate himself and be in a pool of cool water. This frog is thinking it over."

He paused.

"The recipient is about to retire, you see. It's a bit subtle perhaps, but I hope he'll see the various points."

A row of small plastic cups lay on the bench to Laurence's right, each one containing a dark liquid.

"It's a colour test", explained Laurence, "a line-blend of two materials. One at each end. You take equal measures of each for the cup in the middle. Then from the middle cup you mix equal measures with the cups at each end. Then you've got five blends. If you want you can take further intermediate measures, making nine, and so on. Then you fire them on a tile and see the results. The beauty of it is that you only have to weigh the two original quantities. The rest only needs a tea-spoon. Excuse me, please, but I must get on. I'm working to a date."

After looking at the kilns and the clay-processing equipment we returned to the front of the old workshop, where Jaki was dipping a series of pint jugs in a large tub of glaze. Jaki is a lively, attractive red-head, a local girl who came here without any training in ceramics. It was not surprising that someone with her determination became quite a skilled potter and painter in only a short time. She also became a useful administrator, keeping the order book up to date and maintaining the showroom. More surprisingly, she revealed a flair for portait drawing and cartoons and a penchant for astrology. She also took us aback on one occasion by spending all her savings on a lightning trip to California to see the Beach Boys. When she started here she was so shy that she used to hide behind the chimney whenever strangers came in, but her confidence grew and those days are hard to remember.

"You must be the sales-person."

"Not me. There isn't one, really. People have to catch whoever is nearest. Today I'm the one in the hot seat. We take it in turns."

Breaking off in the middle of a job is always tiresome, but selling is not without its importance. Jaki washed the glaze off her hands at the sink and accompanied us up to the showroom. A drumming sound issued from the office at the far end: Stella was typing out an exhibtion list on the heavy Olivetti, an unloved machine that makes the floor shudder.

Our visitor looked through the pottery on display and chose several pieces without hesitation.

"This place has a definite house-style," he commented, "I like it. But now and again I see something that stands apart." He pointed out a jug painted with an owl wearing sun-glasses. "How come?"

Jaki reddened under her freckles.

"That's one of mine. It's a caricature of a friend in L.A.. I did one for him and then I made an extra."

"Why the yellow price-tag?"

"Alan calls it a special. The yellow tags mean the price is higher than normal."

"I'll take it. I've a place for that piece. Why, if it isn't the split image of my wife's uncle Carlos!"

Jaki entered the purchases in the invoice book and took them down to pack. The American turned to me and his reassuring remarks have stayed in my mind ever since. I had felt that my management of the business was too indecisive, yet could not see how it could be done differently. He said that the place looked very different from what one expects in the twentieth century, but it seemed to him to make twentieth century sense. It used people's creative motivation, something which is all too easily lost. He liked what he called our 'soft mortar'. "Hard mortar's aggressive", he said. "You build situations, make business". With the soft kind it comes to you – people, projects, ideas. The rules of the game are different. A big set-up and a small one each have their place and they are quite different. Everyone has to be clear which they want to be.

He passed me his card, Morton J. Barratt, Barratt Construction (Atlanta) Incorporated.

"You'll want some of the binding medium." He smiled and brought out his traveller's cheques. "Even the best mortar fails without this."

We stowed the purchases in his car and waved him off. The visit was well timed; interesting things were going on and the potters responded to him. I enjoyed his appreciation and his comments resolved a tangle in my mind.

The accepted wisdom of the day is that unless an enterprise grows it must be a failure, or is only marking time. Influenced by the prevailing mood, I had at one time increased the numbers from five to ten, plus two part-time helpers, and acquired additional work-space. We made and sold more pottery but the quality of the work declined, the overhead costs increased, and I found myself forced to devote more and more time to transient misunderstandings, with never enough peace for my own work or for new projects. The crisis was accentuated by the onset of rapid inflation and the finances became precarious. Fortunately several people moved on, for other reasons, leaving us at eight, and I did not try to replace them. Our activities were transformed, and eight has remained the usual number ever since.

I had recognised just in time that even a small increase in size can be destructive, that the apparent growth may be an illusion. At a certain critical point it takes the fun out of the work, and when the fun goes the energy goes, so that everyone has to try harder and work longer with less and less effect.

Soon afterwards, *Small is Beautiful* was published. It was a profound reassurance to read that book. Schumacher showed that for every kind of activity there is an ideal size and number. Some things, he said, can only be done on a small scale, and in some areas of work enthusiasm, trust, experience and the qualities of individuals are more important than technology and expansion. I had felt this in my bones, but I could have embraced the man for explaining it and backing it up with his managerial experience.

I have never since been tempted to pass the number eight as a working group. It amounts to much more than eight times one. Oliver Roskill, an old friend of the family and himself a distinguished industrial consultant, called it a magic number in human affairs, providing what he termed "maximum flexibilty for minimum management" and he said it was no accident that it recurs again and again, in committees, in a military section, at a dinner party and in the Boat Race.

The chemistry of people is far subtler than the chemistry of glazes or clay or colours, and the smaller the enterprise the more it matters.

7

LUSTRE

I had no idea how much it involved. I was dreaming of majestic sheens of lustrous crimson and gold remembered from Spanish lustre, though at that time I had seen very little and didn't know how it was made. I was also wanting to extend the range of my ceramic colours. Tin-glaze is admirable for many colours, but strong reds are hard to get, and the best reds come from reduced copper lustre. They do not come easily. It is like the Irishman in the story: "If I'd have told you how far you had to go, you'd never have had the heart to begin."

I knew at that time only two books offering practical guidance on the subject, William Ruscoe's handbook, published in the 1930s, and the *Formulario* of the Catalan ceramist Llorens Artigas. Ruscoe's book contained three lustre recipes; Artigas's notebook contained dozens and also provided instructions for the reduction firings, but I only realised later that they were ideas he meant to try out, not mixtures he had actually tested.

In those days I had only a small electric kiln and unfortunately electric kilns are not really suitable for reduction. It can only be done by pushing combustible materials such as sticks or oil or moth-balls through the spy-hole to use up the oxygen. This is not easy and it's almost impossible to maintain the reduction all through the kiln for more than a few minutes, so I made a kiln-within-a-kiln by knocking a section out of the side of a saggar and placing it upside down opposite the spyhole. It looked like a small house with a doorway. Inside I placed small mugs painted with Ruscoe's recipe and mixtures from the *Formulario*. I heated the kiln until there was a dull red glow inside, as the book said. Then I rolled moth-balls down a slide through the spyhole and into the kiln. They ignited violently and I nearly lost my right eye as a jet of gas shot back through the spyhole. I persevered as long as

I could stand it and then left the kiln to cool. The mugs came out completely unchanged.

Next time I tried with pieces of oily rag. No better. Then I used oily rags and wooden sticks, which maintained the reduction for longer. Unfortunately they also increased the temperature, so that the glaze softened and the clayey pigments adhered to it, making it impossible to rub off the clay 'revealing the film of shining metal' as the books promised. Eventually I had a brainwave. Pieces of fudge, skewered on to a metal rod, could be pushed well inside the upturned saggar. As soon as they began to burn they dripped off, allowing me to insert more. The smell was delicious and I could continue for some time without being gassed. After several attempts at last three mugs came out with definite signs of lustre. I rubbed the clay away and polished the glaze vigorously. There was no doubt of it: one was a dull, metallic red; one was a sheeny brown, and one side of the third mug shone with a metallic orange-gold. If I was not fully hooked before, I was now.

Reduction-firing is easiest with wood or gas. It is simply a matter of restricting the air supply to the burning fuel. The combustion of the wood or gas then uses up all the oxygen inside the kiln and the resulting reducing atmosphere immediately begins to affect the metal based pigments used for decoration or as glaze colourants. Red iron oxide loses one of its oxygen atoms to become ferrous oxide, which is green. Copper oxide, which gives a bright green in a neutral atmosphere, becomes red. This is the basis of the jade green celadons and sang-de-boeuf obtained on stoneware and porcelain and of the low temperature gold red lustres.

At that time we had not yet built a wood-fired kiln. The kiln we constructed the following year would anyway have been far too large for the many small tests that would be needed to understand the lustre process. For these tests we built a miniature wood-fired kiln. The chamber was a cube with sides of about fifteen inches, with a firebox on one side and a small chimmney on the other. It could be heated to between 600-700°C. in about two hours. The first attempts were fun but by the sixteenth attempt, with little to show for the effort, enthusiasm was wearing thin, especially as it had started to snow. Altogether, twenty-six test firings were made in this tiny kiln before we managed to produce anything with any reasonable silver and copper lustre. I still have some of these pieces. It is difficult now to comprehend the awe they aroused or the confidence they inspired. None of us, however, had the faintest idea how much more there was to learn.

It shouldn't have been necessary to have nearly so many test firings. True, one learns better from one's own mistakes than from other people's knowledge, but it would have saved time had there been anyone to consult. Unfortunately the best-informed people were all dead. Later I met in Spain and in Egypt two men whose experience would have helped a great deal, but I only met them because of the work I had already done on my own. I could have prepared myself better by reading de Morgan, Franchet, Burton and others, but at that time I didn't know of their writings, and I might not have learnt much from them without making my own mistakes first.

The test-firings pointed to three basic principles which I never found clearly expressed in writing even when I became better informed.

1. The pigments present little difficulty: almost any mixture of silver and copper compounds with equal weight of clay or ochre can produce a reduced lustre finish. Time is better spent on
2. the composition of the glaze, because only a few earthenware glazes are suitable. The best appear to be fusible compositions rich in sodium. But however suitable the glazes may be they cannot produce good effects unless
3. the firing is correct, with periods of reduction at the right temperature, of the right intensity, and maintained for the right length of time, which depends on the size of the kiln.

I wondered now about firing lustre on a larger scale. The fuel was no problem, since plenty of reject wood was locally available from cricket bat willows. A larger kiln was needed anyway for the regular firings, and I now had just enough help to be able to build one. It took about a year of intermittent work, making and selling pottery to pay our way as we went on. The kiln turned out not particularly suitable for the regular tin-glaze ware, but was remarkably good for lustre.

The procedure was simple. The pots were glazed plain white and painted with mixtures of red clay and compounds of silver and copper. They were placed on shelves and protected from the direct flame by small baffles. The kiln was fired until it glowed dull red. The lowest temperature Seger cones were used: O22, O21 and O20, recording temperatures between 620–660°C. Once the first of the cones had bent the fire was heavily stoked, using up all the air, so that reduction occurred in the kiln chamber. A wavy plume of thick, black smoke rose from the chimney, lasting for about three minutes. As soon as it died down, more wood was thrown on the fire and once again the chimney belched and wisps of smoke issued from every crevice in the brickwork. At intervals, test rings were taken out of the chamber on a long metal rod. Once they showed a sheen of reddish-gold, all the apertures were sealed up and the kiln was left to cool. The temperature was consistently uneven. The upper parts were best for copper reds and the cooler areas best for silver, while silver-copper mixtures were best in the middle.

These early firings were carefree affairs and they were remarkably successful. You can't worry much if you have so little idea of what you ought to be doing. The crackle of the wood, the surge of the flames and the plume of black smoke were fun and it was so exciting to achieve any lustre at all that nobody worried about the things that went wrong.

Some beautiful pieces came out of this haphazard beginning, velvety crimson-reds, brilliant amber-golds of which someone said 'they have the sun in them', a comment one doesn't forget. From the cooler parts of the kiln some silvery-green lustres, a colour I later recognised in early medieval Egyptian pottery. These were effects I had half hoped for, but unexpected things happened too. I had not foreseen the effect of reduction on the glaze. Sometimes the glaze was changed to a soft grey, varying over the surface of the pot, and sometimes lightly speckled like the fine skin of a fish. Here and there, where the flames had played directly on to the pots, the glaze had turned blue-black and the sheen of lustre glowed on it with mysterious intensity. Against this dark ground, the silver pigments became an iridescent steely blue which I had never seen before.

The best surprise was the red vapour-flashing that developed from a blend of silver chloride and copper carbonate. In places where the flames formed a back-eddy the lustre brush-stroke became golden-orange and the copper vapourised, impregnating the glaze with a brilliant, lustrous red which shaded off to a pink blush. The vapour effect transformed the edges of the brush-strokes in ways one could never have planned in advance.

The only cloud on the horizon was that we couldn't sell these nice things. None of the retailers who sold our painted tin-glaze pots were interested in the lustre, even at the lowest possible prices. We had all assumed that our first beautiful lustre could not fail to be a commercial success. It was not.

At times like this friends quarrel and partnerships break up because of the difficulty of balancing enthusiasm with business. There are no right answers. I was glad that I was carrying the financial risk and that I had to decide the matter on my own.

You have to follow your star. Having got this far I could not think of giving up. In my mind's eye I was already seeing glorious things that might one day be made, and I felt sure that eventually the business aspect would take care of itself. A talented friend of mine, also working in ceramics, was once talking about his work to a business man.

"I'm sure this project will succeed in the end," he said. "I know it's good, and besides, no-one else is doing anything like it." "Have you asked yourself why?" said the business man. Two equally valid ways of looking at the same thing.

Sometimes you feel you have been given a Sign. A few weeks after the auspicious lustre-firing I had a visit from Henry Rothschild. Having looked through the lustre he promptly proposed an exhibition at his Primavera gallery in Sloane Street. The lustre was utterly different from the austere, textured stoneware that was generally in vogue at that time, but Henry liked doing the unexpected and he was prepared to take the risk.

Henry had a unique place in the crafts scene. Pioneer of an exciting and respected gallery, he was a natural entrepreneur, a collector, traveller, and critic, and through his German background he was in touch with what was happening in the crafts in Europe generally, not only in Britain. He was always fun and well worth listening to even when he was wrong. Of all the gallery owners I have met, Henry was the only one who could see what someone's work might become as clearly as he saw what it was at the time, and his constructive criticisms were incredibly helpful. I had not exhibited on my own in London before, and his offer was a stroke of fortune. There were already enough tin-glaze pieces to make up half the collection; the rest was to be lustre. To make a good showing we needed another firing.

There was so much to do that the vital kiln was fired only nine days before the exhibition was due to open. Everything was done with particular care. The cones recorded a perfect temperature; the reduction was exactly the same as before, and the test rings looked just right. Why then, when the kiln was unpacked the following day, was everything so pale? From all this work only three pieces were worth considering for the exhibition. In spite of all our care, the kiln must have been too cool and the reduction too weak. The only thing to do was to put everything back and fire it again.

This time the cones were well down and the inside of the kiln glowed distinctly red. Was it too much? The reduction was more intense, and at the end of the firing, to make sure of not repeating the same mistake, I crammed the firebox with fuel and allowed a little air into it so that the fire would continue to smoulder for several hours, like a charcoal-burners' clamp.

The pots were certainly not underfired this time. On some the white glaze had turned almost black and on others the clay in the pigment had fused into the glaze and could not be rubbed away, but some of the work came out with a mysterious, iridescent lustre breaking to blue and purple. The glaze had changed from white to speckled grey and steely black, quite unlike the brightness of classic lustre and more

LUSTRE

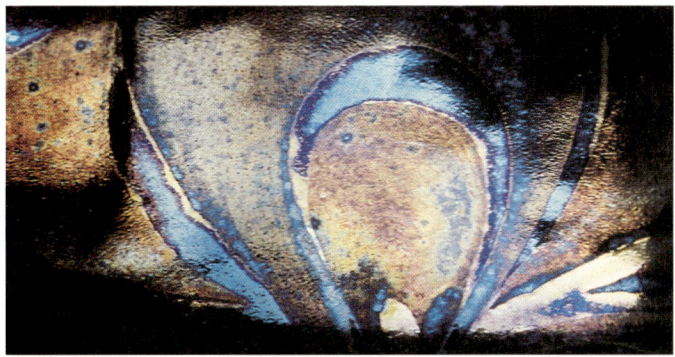

Top: Close-up of vapoured lustre.
Centre: Rubbing down pots after lustre firing: (from left) Gill Bent, Jenny Jowett, Visitor, Catherine Bennett, Miranda Thomas.
Bottom: Large lidded jar, 1975. Large bowl, red and golden lustre, ACS 1994.

like a colour-symphony from the underworld. From lower in the kiln came three bowls with golden lustre flashed with fiery red vapour and from the coolest positions some deep silvery-green. Forty per cent or so of the work was lost but the rest more than made up for it. The question was no longer what to reserve for the exhibition but what to leave out. It all looked wonderfully assured under the bright lights in the gallery in Sloane Street, and the exhibition was an entire success. It was only when Henry embarassed me by announcing the value of the sales at the top of his voice that I realised how doubtful he had been.

Though I have kept detailed records of every firing ever since, and have often exactly repeated the programme of a previous firing, I have been taken by surprise again and again. There are so many variables in a lustre firing, and the margin of error is so fine, that the same thing hardly ever happens twice. Clement Wedgwood came to the same conclusion when he tried it out back in the 1860s, hoping to add it to the Wedgwood range, but he eventually decided it was too unpredictable.

I had begun lustre mainly because it was a way of widening the range of available colours, but the Primavera exhibition showed that here was something far more interesting than simply an extension of the colours. Reduction-lustre reflects iridescent light; at its best it has an emotional key unlike any other kind of colour. I have seen people actually tremble in response to it. Like the vibrations of certain musical instruments, it can reach a frontier of the mind where sensation is scarcely distinguishable from symbol or light from life. The desire to enter this realm can border on obsession.

This may sound a little over the top, but in truth it isn't. It is the kind of motive force that makes things happen. Nor is it just personal. It has surfaced at many different times and places over the ages and its devotees understand one another.

I began to think of forms and painted designs specifically for lustre, instead of simply applying lustre to the forms already current. A new range of designs with flowing calligraphic strokes seemed to be unfolding. At the same time I continued to experiment with new pigments and new glazes, hoping to find compositions suitable for the variable conditions in different parts of the kiln.

Now we all worked together on a new design for a larger wood-fired kiln, incorporating many lessons we had learnt from the first one. Over several months the first kiln was dismantled and the new kiln began to rise up on the enlarged foundations. It worked excellently and has been fired about every five weeks for nearly thirty years since, but it affected the lustre very differently. I was not prepared for the dismal objects that came out of the first two firings in the beautiful new kiln. The colour was pale and starved-looking and the white glazes were a uniform, dreary grey. No brightness, no glory.

During the next seven years enough good things came from the kiln to sustain enough hope to persevere, but the rate of loss was desperately high, about 70%. I simply could not explain why the firings in the old kiln had been so successful. I pored over my records time and again, trying to grasp the secret, but still only a handful of good pieces emerged from each firing. The firings became less and less frequent. Only in 1975, after about eight years, did I begin to read the clues.

The best things, less grey and with stronger lustre, came from the area from which the test-rings were extracted. These rings were hooked out on a long thin iron rod towards the end of the firing, and to get at them you had to remove a small brick in the door, allowing some air into that part of the kiln. I used to do this as quickly as possible, supposing that the air would spoil the lustre by re-oxidising it. But this was in fact the clue. One evening, after yet another disappointing firing, I was re-reading Piccolpasso's *Three Books of the Potter's Art*, the first major European book on pottery, with a view to editing a new publication of the work. I read once again what he had been told by Vincenzo Andreoli of Gubbio in 1557.

> The fuel for it should be straw or else willow-branches, well dried and free from damp; keep up the fire with these for three hours, after which, and already the kiln will be beginning to show a certain glow, take broom or spartium, as Dioscorides calls it, well dried and seasoned, and leaving off the willow give it an hour of fire with this.[1]

Now broom is a bulky material and the furnace could only have been re-fuelled if the previous charge of fuel had died down. There must therefore have been a period of oxidation or relatively clear burning before the next period of reduction. This would affect the kiln as a whole in the same way that a small area was affected when I withdrew the test-rings. It meant that the lustre depended not simply on reduction but on alternating periods of reduction and oxidation in the later stages of the firing. It is obvious, so obvious, once you see it, but it is not explained in any of the technical books (though it is now,)[2] and it was Piccolpasso's discourse of four centuries ago that made it clear.

After this the firings really became effective. A full minute of clear burning was allowed between each spasm of smoky, reducing fire. Repeated seven or eight times, the process lasted nearly an hour and was sufficient to develop the lustre throughout the 160 cubic foot kiln. It was left to cool for two days before the pots were taken out to be washed and rubbed clean of ochre to reveal the lustre. This was a joyful job and it took three or four people a whole day. Although the effect had already developed inside the kiln, everyone felt as if the lustre was actually coming into existence as they polished it, like Aladdin and his lamp.

There followed seven fat years for the lustre, from 1977 to 1984, during which came the big jars for the British Embassy in Washington, the Oxford exhibition of 1979, the successful Sydney exhibition of 1981, most of the lustre for the retrospective exhibition of 1985-87, as well as a large number of commissioned pieces and pots privately purchased. During the same period I wrote *Lustre Pottery*, published by Fabers in 1985. A working potter cannot undertake much original historical research but he can look afresh at what is already known and offer some insights into how things were made and what they mean. The sections on technique, however, and the questions and answers written with Frank Hamer, were almost entirely new and arose from first-hand experience. In them the difficulties of the earlier years bore fruit, for by this time a number of other people had begun to work with lustre, aware of its qualities as a non-industrial medium.

My technical chapters may sound more authoritative than I actually felt, and perhaps the gods saw the book and decided to teach the author a lesson. Things soon began to go wrong again, but by now the theory and practice had come together. After a painful period of wasteful effort I re-read my own chapters in *Lustre Pottery*. It is strange to realise that in the press of activity one can forget one's own knowledge. Only when I carefully studied what I had written several years before did I understand what was going wrong and find the solution.

Remembering the Irishman, I wonder now if I would ever have begun if I had known how far there was to travel. The same question could be asked about everything people try to do. Fortunately no-one can see the whole distance in advance and we have to tackle it in a kinder way, week by week and moment by moment.

8

SAID EL SADR

I had wanted for a long time to see the lustres in the Islamic Museum in Cairo, but Egypt is far away and I kept postponing the trip because of new commitments near at hand. What tipped the balance was a major exhibition of medieval Islamic art in 1969, a unique event celebrating the thousandth anniversary of the foundation of the city. It was a must.

The Islamic Museum is well known to connoisseurs and historians but at that time tourists seldom even heard of it. Anyway it was the era of Nasser and Brehznev and the hotels were full of bored Russian technicians and trade representatives, though how anyone could find Cairo boring is beyond me.

The streets leading to the Museum were pot-holed and puddled with liquid from drains and decomposing garbage, but the traders' stalls were bright with fruit and vegetables and lively with the cries and theatrical gestures that always accompany buying and selling. A strange assortment of vapours hung in the air, horse-dung and diesel fumes, joss-sticks, fruits. sewage, tobacco, leather and wood-smoke.

Inside the Museum all was dim and silent and there was no sign of any staff or visitors. I felt like an intruder in a deserted palace, wandering amongst carpets, silks, painted woodwork, immense doors carved with mind-bending 'everlasting designs', marquetry, blown glass enamelled and gilded, palace vessels of gold and silver, bronze, brass and steel with intricate inlaid figures; mihrabs and pilasters and tiles with Koranic inscriptions, and, of course, ceramics of many kinds , amongst which were the lustres of the Fatimid dynasty of the eleventh and twelfth century that I had come to see.

The variety and joie de vivre of the lustres took me by surprise, shining with silver-green and sun-gold images of people and animals, floriated inscriptions, scrolls and fruits, and ingenious geometric designs. They breathed the life of a world I knew nothing about yet there was something strangely familiar about them. I passed an hour or two enjoying them and making sketches, completely absorbed, until a custodian arrived on the scene and took news of my arrival to Madame Waffiya Izzi, the Director.

She was in all respects the largest lady I had ever met, and was generous in equal measure. She was also a devoted scholar, familiar with every object in her charge, and during the next few days I received through her thoughtful kindness far more than I could ever have asked for. Now, clapping her hands, she summoned two of the custodians who squatted in the corridor outside and ordered coffee. The thick, sweet liquid was brewed in copper vessels over a small charcoal brazier placed on broken tiles in the corridor. She clapped again; a third man appeared and was sent to fetch Abd'l Rauf, the keeper of the ceramics.

He was in those days a thin, dark-skinned man in his late thirties, an industrious archaeologist and scholar. He brought out other ceramics from the reserves and explained the background of the objects I had been recording, especially the interconnections between different arts during the extraordinary rule of the Fatimid caliphs. From my questions he saw that I had some experience of firing lustre.

"He must meet El Sadr", they said to each other. They explained. "He works at Fustat, where they made lustre in medieval times."

We telephoned. Next day I met Said el Sadr outside the mosque of Amr el As on the southern edge of old Cairo. We drove in his ancient VW to his studio at Fustat.

Fustat was half wasteland. The dry, stony earth was dotted with clay sherds from centuries of manufacture going right back to Roman times. There were about two dozen workshop-compounds with rough walls built of brick, pots, and limestone held together with mortar and clay. Some were family workshops enclosing stores of materials, wheels and simple equipment, and in some cases the family dwelling. Others were large enough to accomodate perhaps half a dozen workers and included open spaces where the pots were lined up to dry or to wait for finishing. These had no living-area, only a den for the watchman and the guard-dog.

El Sadr's compound was one of the smallest but it had stone walls. The arch over the entrance was inscribed in Arabic and English 'El Sadr Ceramic Centre, Fustat'. We passed through into a courtyard. A small child and some hens were scratching in the dust. To the left of the entrance was a lean-to shed, where the caretaker lived. He appeared, clad in a dirt-stained galabeia, and moved the child out of the way, depositing it behind a small kiln made of broken pots and old bricks tacked together

SAID EL SADR

with mud, which stood in front of the dwelling.

"My man", remarked El Sadr as we walked past.

Across the compound was a shaded, open-sided area with a tiled floor, two potter's wheels, a bench and shelves of pots and modelled figures in various stages of completion. In front of us stood the main studio, a square room with windows facing into the the courtyard and an awning to shade the sun. Inside was a little fireplace, shelves, benches, tables and two chairs. Every surface was filled with pots or painting materials, drawings, jars, bowls, books, photographs and trial-pieces, all covered with a film of the sandy dust that settles on everything all over Egypt. In the middle of a wide table stood a bowl of fresh fruit. El Sadr cleared a space and put water to boil on a paraffin stove for coffee.

He was a large, vigorous man of about sixty, heavily built and with a slightly unsteady gait. His face was powerful and deeply lined and his dark eyes glowed. He spoke fluent English, with a strong Arabic accent. He would listen attentively and then break into a slow smile, followed by sudden laughter and an emphatic comment.

We talked over the table with coffee and cigarettes. I showed him my photographs and a few pieces of lustre I had brought with me. He brought out pots and figures made from the local earthenware clays, and various kinds of lustre that he had recently fired in the small kiln in the yard.

"The firing is not with wood. You see, we have not enough. It is with straw of sugar cane. But the reduction is with leather. Yes, leather and rubber. Old shoes! Rubbish. Of that we have very much! You have seen it." He made a sweeping gesture to indicate a hill, and I remembered the vast mounds we passed on our way to the studio, where women and children and goats were picking over the sun-dried refuse. "They collect things for many people. For me, old shoes!"

El Sadr had experimented extensively. As well as tin-glaze lustres similar to my own, he showed me reduced in-glaze lustres based upon copper and iron, lustres on black glazes, lustres over coloured engobes, and reduced turquoise glazes painted with animals and human figures in an unusual combination of red lustre and turquoise green. He was particularly pleased with these pieces. He leaned towards me.

"This you have never seen!"

The copper in the turquoise glaze had turned golden-red in the firing. On this surface he painted designs in molten wax. The piece was then dipped in hydrofluoric acid, which dissolved the red surface of the glaze and exposed the lower layer, which remained the original colour. The wax was then removed with hot water, revealing the design in red against the turquoise ground. The effect was lively and ingenious. Characteristically, he never mentioned that hydrofluoric acid is highly dangerous.

Everything El Sadr did was inventive and charged with feeling. He was an all-round artist, painter, sculptor, and draughtsman as well as potter and ceramist. He had spent a few years in England in the mid 1930s, painting and working with Bernard Leach at St Ives, and he also studied at Camberwell, experimenting with reduced lustres. Unfortunately he got little encouragement and gave up the project, but returned to it later in Egypt, inspired by the same medieval lustres I had seen in the Museum.

"In Egypt we have an important school of ceramics," he said. "It began here at Fustat eight centuries ago. It is truly Islamic, and it is also universal. Six centuries ago the potters had to abandon it – for political reasons – but their vision is still alive. In my work it continues to unfold. There are many things they had not time to do when they were prevented. I develop this vision."

He paused, the heavy features of his face relaxed, gazing downward. The room was lit lustrous gold by the descending sun.

Suddenly he looked up fiercely.

"Why do the potters of the West know nothing of this? They study, they travel, they understand many things. But of this school of ceramics they know nothing." He paused. "You are the only one to come."

We met again outside the mosque next day. Walking to the studio, we passed some small boys in grubby galabeias, scampering in and out of one of the workshops as they placed newly made pots in the sun to dry. They were about twelve years old. I asked if they went to school. El Sadr shook his head.

"Here at least they learn something."

We visited several family workshops. He knew everyone and I was introduced to a great many potters. He said it was important for them to meet someone from the West who could appreciate what they did. Many foreigners came to Egypt but they did not see these people.

He also showed me a number of the rounded, hump-backed kilns, which are fired with sugar cane straw through an arched tunnel that leads into the furnace. They were like beautiful sculptures. El Sadr suddenly became very excited.

These you must photograph".

I had no camera.

"You are the first for fifty years to come to Egypt without a camera! Take mine." The absurdity delighted him.

SAID EL SADR

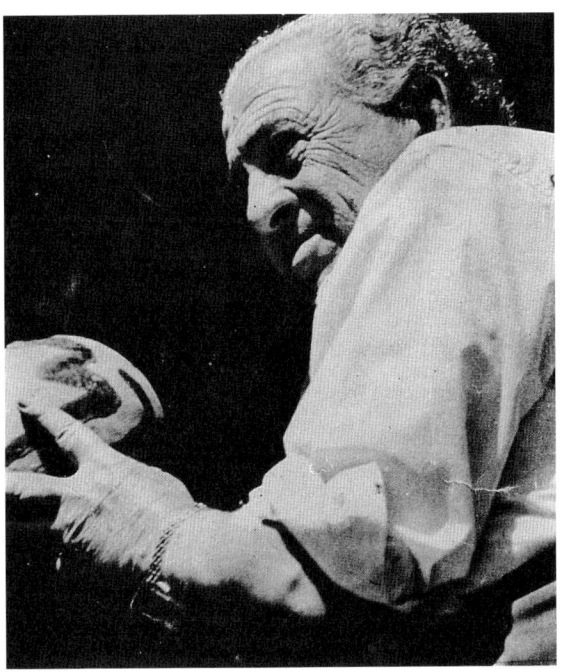

Top: Said El Sadr, about 1979.
Bottom: "Here at least they learn something."

That evening he said, "Your work is of the West, but of all that Western work in ceramics only yours is concerned with our heritage. You will hold here a big exhibition. It will be in the Semiramis. Our young artists will understand that they do not have to follow the East or London or New York because there exists in the West a manifestation of our school of lustre ceramics. This they must know. I shall speak of this exhibition to the Minister. He is my friend. It will be arranged."

Like everything El Sadr said, it was emphatic and wide open to disappointment. I had already seen enough of Egypt to know that this exhibition would never happen. I wondered whether he believed in it himself. So far as I was concerned something wonderful had happened already. It was as if we had been expecting each other.

We spent several days together. Amongst other things we visited the University, where he had recently been Dean of the Faculty of Fine Art, and he showed me some impressive diploma exhibitions. There was no doubt of his devotion to young Egyptian artists nor of his conviction, not shared by many of his contemporaries, that this was a vital growing point for his country. Evidently he had resigned from his post after a major row with the Education Minister, who wished the teaching to have more industrial emphasis. This was for political reasons, he said. He regarded all economic and political matters as an interruption in the serious artistic work of the people, be it the war with Israel or the Soviet technology then being poured into the country, or the British presence during the two world wars, or the Ottoman domination, or the overthrow of the Fatimid caliphs by the Ayyubids, or the Roman occupation in the first century B.C. "These are interruptions, sometimes long waves, sometimes short waves," he said. "They interfere with the creative work which is in the heart of the people. The Roman Empire. In that time they were very much disturbed."

After resigning, he built his studio compound at Fustat in the midst of the potteries. They produced vast quantities of unglazed water-pots, molasses-jars, planters, pitchers, lamps and storage jars, and also drainpipes, floor tiles and facing bricks. The potters made these things with breathtaking fluency, but like many traditional artisans they were too good at it, and too busy, to conceive of changing anything. El Sadr knew they were in a poverty trap. Year by year the demand for their products diminished as the world around them changed. They lowered their prices and worked harder, all to no avail. El Sadr said they had the ability to be artists as well as artisans. "This they must follow, or they die."

"They are simple men," he went on. "They cannot read. They do not analyse. You cannot teach them as you teach in the school. But as I work they will see new forms, they will see the colours, the glazes, the lustres. They will ask questions. Then I can help them."

El Sadr was devoted to Fustat and its potters and he appeared to know everyone. His little book *Medinat al Fukhar*, (*The Town of the Potters*) published in Arabic in 1967, was an attempt to gain recognition for them. Again he was positive and emphatic, though wide open as ever to disappointment. He was trying to achieve a new break for the potters, comparable to what Wissa Wassif did for the tapestry-makers of Haraneya, but the unit value of tapestries is relatively very high and they make better sense in modern interiors. El Sadr's hopes depended on radical retraining and a considerable marketing organisation. One man alone could not do it.

When I returned to Fustat ten years later, half the potteries had disappeared and in their place were kilns burning lime for cement and foundries for recycling waste metal. A new road, used mostly by heavy construction vehicles, cut across the slope below El Sadr's Ceramic Centre. The remaining potteries were working just as before and there was no sign of anything new. El Sadr did not refer to his earlier hopes. Instead he said,

"Alan, you will establish the International Group of Lustre Ceramicists! I shall be the senior member. Peascod and Oldroyd and Nabil Darwish and others will join us. We shall hold exhibitions, arrange conferences. This is important. The people will come. It will grow."

I hadn't the heart to say it, but I felt sure that for political reasons, if for no other, these hopes would be 'prevented'.

El Sadr's hopes for Fustat are unlikely to be fulfilled, but his longing to breathe new life into lustre has not been entirely disappointed. He taught me a great deal, and in practice and in writing I have passed on much that came from him. He also communicated his spirit to Alan Peascod, who came from Australia to study with him at Fustat and later became a major force in one of the most enterprising ceramic communities in the modern world. El Sadr himself visited Australia and, though his idiosyncracies and disregard of clock time were not pleasing to the authorities, his ideas and practical methods were an oasis for many students. It could no longer be said that the West knows nothing of the heritage of the Fatimid lustre makers, though their legacy will never again appear in the same form because the world has changed. The seeds have blown a long way on the wind and some have fallen on good ground. Who knows what will happen next? We have no more control over the future than the artisans of Fustat.

The sole survivor.

9

ASHTRAYS

In the early days money was tight and the future was unpredictable. There was a certain glamour about that time, at least in retrospect. We jumped at the chance of any order that might keep the business afloat.

The order in this case was was for thirty ashtrays at 12s.6d. each plus 15% purchase tax. They were for the George Hotel, Pangbourne, near where Kenneth Grahame wrote the *Wind in the Willows*. Many details of the locality feature in the book. Toad Hall is supposed to be based on a stockbroker's riverside mansion and local tradition says that the collapsed timbers over an inlet above the weir are the remains of Ratty's boat-house.

The flat rims of the ashtrays were to have two recesses for cigarettes, with the name and telephone number of the hotel inscribed between them, and the concave middle was to be decorated either with emblems of St. George, or with Mole, Ratty and Toad in scenes from the *Wind in the Willows*.

"The more colourful the better," said our customer. "They have to catch the eye. The hotel guests will pinch them, of course. That's a good advertisement, and it means we shall need more in the near future."

It was difficult to record the details in the order book because he kept talking. He ended by saying he would be back from the South of France in a month's time and expected the ashtrays to be ready by then.

Our visitor was a substantial man in his late fifties, hooded in an immense overcoat with a wide astrakan collar. His balding head was covered by a large Homburg hat and he carried light tan leather gloves and a stick. His wide face had the flush of good living and he smelt of expensive after-shave. He cut an incongruous figure on the narrow steps leading up to the showroom. He was eminently dislikeable, but the scent of business made us eager to please him.

He said he was a director of the Twenty-first Century Company, with offices in London, Dusseldorf and Nice. They had a good many hotels. The George was a new acquisition and they were just beginning to make something of it.

I accompanied him to the door. Outside stood a superb cream-coloured, vintage Rolls Royce with tinted windows and lemon-yellow leather upholstery.

"Another recent acquisition", he explained as I admired it, "originally tailor-made for a fine lady in merchant banking. A useful gadabout."

He drove off.

The name on the order-sheet was E. Wasslow-Merrett.

"It's probably not his real name," said Judith. "I wouldn't trust that man an inch, and I'm sure there's no such thing as the Twenty-first Century Company."

"The Rolls is real," said David. "That's good enough for me. Let's get on with the job."

To get a co-operative workshop off the ground one needs to build up everyone's skill and generate a sense of responsibility and participation. There were only four of us working together in those days and it was agreed that we would each work out some designs and make prototypes of the best ones.

Edgar came up with a design of St George on his war-horse, side view, wearing a great deal of armour and holding a lance. Extensive patterned blankets covered the horse's flanks and extended some way down its legs, making it, in his own words, "less hellish to draw."

David produced a dramatic version of St George seen from the front, about to thrust his lance into the dragon's gaping throat, which threatened to engulf him from below. David was a mysterious character and I had not realised he could draw like this. Sometimes he wouldn't speak for two or three days on end. At other times he would engage in long and well-informed discussions of abstruse historical or scientific questions. He spent most of his spare time shut up in his cottage, every now and again emerging with a perfectly finished picture or a humourous piece of writing.

Judith promised nothing. She said this kind of thing wasn't her line at all, and anyway she wouldn't dream of doing anything for such a vile man. But she consented to do the inscriptions.

I worked out a design showing St George airborne on a leaping horse, thrusting his lance downward into the mouth of a dragon reminiscent of the mouth of hell in medieval wall-paintings. The horse and rider stood out against a background of sulphur-yellow fumes. I would have liked to include the princess whom St George rescues, but in a dish only seven inches wide there wasn't room.

Most of the protopye ashtrays came out well. Encouraged by this success, I designed and painted two more, showing the mole and the water rat in a small boat under an overhanging willow branch. Ratty was rowing and mole sat nervously in the stern, as if crying out "Oh my, Oh my...", as it says in the book. The boat should have been blue, but I made it red, remembering that we had been told to make the designs as colourful as we could. We were looking forward to showing off the fruits of our labour.

Mr. Wasslow-Merrett reappeared a month later. He approved of the ashtrays but his reaction was something of an anticlimax. He said they would 'walk' pretty quickly, but he didn't examine them closely or notice the details. He doubled the order, however, suggesting that there should be another design showing Toad in his new car, or standing in front of Toad Hall. However, he maintained that 12s.6d. was too much and that 10s.0d. would be more appropriate, since he was also going to have to pay 15% purchase tax.

This had to be accepted. We had done most of the time-consuming design work already and it would be a shame to lose the order at this stage. Wasslow-Merrett paid in cash for the seven ashtrays already completed, expressing the hope that the first half of the order would soon be completed, since the hotel was already going places.

The first thirty ashtrays were completed as quickly as possible, and delivered to the hotel. Amongst them was the new design, showing Toad with goggles and big driving gloves standing on the drive leading to the portico of Toad Hall. I had great fun doing it and hoped it would not be stolen before the hotel guests had time to enjoy it. When I arrived at the hotel the receptionist said that Mr. Wasslow-Merrett was not available. Apparently he was in Germany. It was disappointing, as I had hoped to be paid on the spot.

The barman who received our boxes appeared to know nothing about any order for ashtrays. He was so off-hand that I decided not to leave the invoice with him in case it got lost. Later that day I typed it out to make it look more official and sent it by post.

It made little difference. It was never paid at all, though we had to pay the purchase tax on it to the Customs and Excise, since at that time there was no redress for unpaid debts.

After submitting the bill several times without effect, I visited the George to present it in person, intending to take back the ashtrays if no payment could be obtained. Mr. Wasslow-Merrett was said to be in Portugal. I looked around; there was no sign of any ashtrays. Eventually I went to the bar and found the man who had originally taken in the boxes.

"Ah those" he said wistfully. "That was a long time ago. I didn't see much of them. They were all nicked in the first ten days. Too bad."

"But good advertising", I ventured.

"Do we need it?" He flicked his duster and went on polishing the counter.

John King was retired from the diplomatic service. He had a small farm and an orchard near Pangbourne. A few weeks after my visit to the George he called at the Pottery to collect some armorial dishes we had made for him and he happened to notice one of the prototype ashtrays.

"As a matter of interest," he asked, "Did you get paid?"

"Unfortunately not."

"Nor did I. He owed me for poultry and eggs and fruit. It came to quite a lot. He went bankrupt last April, you know. He was tried for fraud, in connection with a false prospectus for raising bank loans in France. It was in the papers. The trial came up in Marseilles, but he died of a heart attack before they finished the hearing."

He wrote out his cheque and turned to leave.

"He used several names, you know. They were apt to change according to the time of day. The real one was Williams."

We could hear Judith laughing.

10

GIPSY BOWLS

He was a real Gipsy, with a horse and a painted cart. I supposed he was looking for scrap iron or had come to sell us besoms or firewood. Many Gipsies came to this area because it is near the county boundary, and they quite often called at our door.

This man, however, was buying not selling and he placed an order: he wanted to give his wife a pair of deep, rounded bowls holding half a gallon, decorated in as many colours as possible inside, outside and underneath the foot, "to keep them safe".

This last remark caught my fancy. The more I saw of decorated pottery from the past, the more convinced I became that it was not just done to please. The patterns and emblems were invocations of happiness and prosperity, talismans of gratitude to keep the vessel and its contents and its users free from harm, and the pots belonged to a way of living in which everything had a meaning. Today we have almost lost the language of emblems and images and designs are usually regarded simply as aesthetic ornament. The very idea that they could mean anything is considered odd. I believe the colours too once had meanings; green, red, blue and gold, were not just expressions of personal taste but had specific significance.

Anyway, I felt this about my own painted designs and colours, and I wanted them to develop the resonance and conviction that I found in pots from long ago. So when the Gipsy gave his unexpected request for the bowls to be painted underneath to keep them safe, I warmed to him as one of the rare old kind who still understood what 'decoration' was really about.

In matters of importance Gipsies usually keep their word, but naturally he had not left an address and it crossed my mind that he might not return. He was a likeable man and it would be disappointing if he didn't, but it wouldn't really matter. In any case the idea appealed to me so much that I treated the bowls as a labour of love and made several extras for my own pleasure. While they were waiting a number of people took

Top: A poem bowl: Venetia Sieveking, 1975.
Centre: Fox and Hounds bowl: Laurence McGowan, 1978.
Bottom: Jonah bowl: ACS, 1995.

a fancy to them; all the extras were soon sold and several similar pots were ordered. I enjoyed explaining how the idea had come about, and before long gipsy bowls became a popular category in the Pottery's repertoire.

Nearly two years passed before the horse and cart once again drew up at the door. The Gipsy was delighted. He said the pots were 'a perfect job' and paid on the nail.

The gipsy bowls took a new turn when Venetia came. She was the daughter of an old friend and she wanted work for a few months before going abroad on a Churchill Scholarship. I took her on as a general helper, although she was a painter by training and had no knowledge of pottery. She found it difficult to adapt her painting technique to our calligraphic designs and at first there wasn't much for her to do. The gipsy bowls offered a solution. There were a number of biscuit-fired bowls ready and waiting. There was no fixed design for these pots and she could paint on them in her own manner, working out her own themes. She said the only trouble was that she couldn't think how to begin. Then we hit on an idea that could keep her happy for weeks.

The idea was that she should take a favourite poem as a starting point and use the colours and motifs suggested by it as the underlying theme of the design. It wouldn't be in any way an illustration; there was no need for figurative imagery; she could think of it as an abstract painting in the round, inside and outside the bowl, using whatever the poem brought into her mind.

It worked. Starting with Kubla Khan and Macbeth's 'Out, out brief candle' Venetia was happily engaged for months on a series of gipsy bowls, each of which became a unique, self-contained world, with visual equivalents of the poems inside, outside and underneath. She was off on a voyage of discovery, but she was still available for odd jobs when she was needed.

I have never seen anything quite like these elaborately painted bowls. The design extended around the bowl without any repetition, outside and inside, a continually changing sequence of shapes and colours, varying in scale and detail, all brought together by the unifying theme of the poem. One was aware of this focal point but since the poem was not directly referred to, the theme remained open and slightly mysterious. This suited Venetia well. Figurative painting was not her line but she was extremely inventive in other ways. It would be difficult to guess what the poems were, and there was no need to do so, but if you were given the key you could detect them within the her colourful, semi-abstract compositions. The ten or so bowls she produced during the next months sold unexpectedly well and I am sorry now that we kept only one.

The poem-bowl sequence might have developed indefinitely except that the time came for Venetia to depart to Iran to study mosque architecture in Isfahan.

Other things happened instead. Next time it was the poem itself. The poem 'Earth circles the brim' was specially composed by John Moat to be inscribed around an earthenware form. The placing had to be carefully considered and the lettering required a skilled calligrapher, so I put John in touch with Madeleine Dinkel. He wrote the poem, I made the pot, and Madeleine inscribed it supremely well. It was a satisfying collaboration for all of us, and the finished piece had a particular point which John must have foreseen, but it was new to me. From a sheet of paper, a short, reflective poem like this can easily be read too fast, but in this form you have to take the bowl in your hands and turn it around, taking in the words unusually slowly and sensing their overtones. The three-dimensional form gave them space and time.

Harriet Owen was the next to get into gipsy bowls. She said she couldn't start from poems, but she would like to have a go with some of her dreams. This led to a succession of unexpected images: Russian Roulette, Goldilocks and the three bears, the Queens of Hearts and Spades, a nightmare, and a fruit-and leaf theme which came from harvesting grapes in a kibbutz, where the foreman used to shout "pick, pick, faster pick, and double-pick".

Harriet was right about doing her dreams. Her intuitive, impetuous nature enabled her to capture the multi-layered imagery of dreams without bothering about where it came from or what it might mean. The owners of her bowls enjoyed trying to interpret them.

Two years later Laurence McGowan gave the idea a new turn. Before taking up ceramics, Laurence had done aerial survey work in Canada and Colombia and then worked as a game-keeper in the New Forest. He had a fine sense of calligraphic design and a rare touch with animals, in art and in active life. Amongst other things he produced a bowl painted with hounds running around the sides and the fox peacefully curled up inside. He also made a memorable inscribed bowl with magpies, from the song "One for sorrow two for joy", with a magpie's nest and eggs in the inside and magpie footprints painted under the foot ring, and the unusual ending "...madam will you dance, seven for old England and eight for France." We should never have sold it.

As a form the gipsy bowl is attractive and holdable and after Laurence left to set up his own studio we produced a number of decorated bowls without special themes. Many of these were made by Andrew Hazelden, whose dancing brushwork gave them a joyful mood, but after the previous bowls one could not help having a sense of a missed opportunity. This changed as soon as Andrew got on to hares. He had never seen a hare until he came to Aldermaston, where they are plentiful, and they fascinated him. Hares began to appear on many of his pots, and best of all on the gipsy bowls. Andrew made some beautiful hare bowls in blue and smoky-golden lustre, and these led on to a Christmas night theme in red lustre with blue and green with hares, deer and other creatures in a forest of star-trees and star-clouds.

Hitherto, the nearest I had come to painting a theme on a gipsy bowl was the 'gods in the forest' bowl, inspired by the giant panga ferns in a New Zealand forest and totem-like forms suggested by Maori tiki figures. Now, seeing what Andrew had done, I did some completely figurative subjects. It was a nice change to attend continuously to a single piece after doing production work. The Jonah bowl was one of the results. The design started from the figure of Jonah relaxing under the gourd, waiting for the fall of Nineveh, and it extended in a dream-like way around the form, ending with the eye of the great fish. I departed completely from Venetia's non-figurative approach and used the roundness of the bowl for a series of images floating into one another.

The next bowl has not yet been completed. I am working from the last stanza of Yeats's poem Byzantium, which is filled with astonishing images, ending with "those dolphin-torn, those gong-tormented seas". I don't fully understand the poem, but that may not matter. One 'reads' these bowls intuitively and the circular sequence of images allows the imagination time to take them in.

Having spent years working on abstract and calligraphic brushwork, it was delightful to rediscover how satisfying imagery and narrative can be on ceramic forms. 'Rediscover' is the key word, for the enjoyment must have been very familiar to the lustre-painters of Kashan and medieval Cairo and of course to the Italian masters of the *istoriato* wares of the Renaissance. Our ventures were a far cry from the lifelong expertise of these specialists, but they nevertheless touched a pulse that belongs essentially to image-making and is not found in other kinds of ceramic painting.

One of the special chacteristics of these bowls is that the painting is on the outside of a circular form which has to be turned in order to see what comes next. Thus it is quite different from the formal, all-in-one eyeful of Italian maiolica dishes. You cannot see it all at once. Instead there is uncertainty and expectation. The whole story of these bowls has been rather like that, never knowing what will come next. Certainly we never foresaw what would happen as a result of the Gipsy's horse and cart drawing up long ago outside the door, and we haven't yet reached the end of it.

"The clay population round in rows": owl mugs and other vessels.

11

ART OR CRAFT

Christmas is coming. Today we put up bunches of holly and mistletoe from the garden and the string of lights in the window, and the showroom is gleaming with finished work. We had an extra wood-firing in November so there's plenty to choose from. The shelves of work in progress are also full. This evening I needed to fetch some papers after the others had gone home. The workshop was warm and the clay population softened the sound of my steps and seemed to fill the empty building with silent communications – jugs, pipkins, plates, casseroles, goblets, vases, platters, jars and bowls of different shapes and sizes, all in various stages of completion. I saw the dark, sheeny-surfaced clay of the pots thrown in the afternoon; the paler, dulled finish of the pots that were drying; the orange-surfaced biscuitware, and the soft white of pots dipped in glaze for painting, all waiting in rows for tomorrow. Even when the workshop is silent it remains full of life.

Omar Khayyam coined the expression 'the clay population round in rows', but pots must have been likened to people from time immemorial. The convention of describing them in terms of the human body is taken for granted. It seems natural they have a foot, a lip, a mouth, shoulder and belly, that they should be waisted or full-bodied or tall-necked. Equally naturally, pots are described as families, like 'famille rose' and' famille verte' because each member of a family originates from the same store of what you might call 'ceramic genes'. The clay, the glaze, the pigments and the firing temperature are the same for all the various vessels in the family, however different in size and shape, and each vessel is formed by the same store of human skills and the pattern of work and human relationships belonging to one particular place. In all kinds of ways, many of which the makers are unaware of, the vessels show their family characteristics. It is as true today as it was of the potters of Valencia, Khorasan and Arita.

Passing through the pottery in the quiet of the evening, wondering at the number of pots that have been added in the last few days, I was reminded of the Hindu symbol of the universal tree, its radiating branches and twigs clothed with the 'manifest creation' of innumerable leaves, all sharing common features but every one unique. The symbol is traditionally applied to all life; the leaves are individual lives in their patch of space and time, and somewhere amongst them is each one of us. But it applies on other scales as well, and at that moment it said something about the pots around me, all obviously members of the same family.

The symbol of the tree suggested something that occurs in all manufacture, whether hand-work or mechanised, a process that could be termed 'Many from One'. That is, the production of a variety of articles that all originate in the same reserve of skills and ideas. The designs can be multiplied or modified without any radical change in the original reserve. Though the range of products increases in the course of time, they all retain certain family features and the manufacture can be done by anyone with the necessary technical skill. One sees this in almost all manufactured things, motor vehicles and books and clothes and computers as well as pottery.

The Fine Arts represent an opposite process, 'One from Many', bringing together a variety of concepts, images and experiences to make a one new, complete whole. In this field, energy spent on repeating or multiplying the products is wasted and may even be destructive since it can prevent something new from taking shape. That's why the work can't easily be shared, and why artists often refuse to repeat something they have already done, whereas a craftsman would probably be glad to do so. Picasso used to say that he took any new thing he wanted from other people's work, but he had a horror of copying himself.

Of course creative artists build on experience and no work, however new, is a completely fresh start. Equally, it would be absurd to suggest that a silversmith or a potter never responds afresh to a new idea. All the same, there is a real difference between the fine artist uniting many elements in a single complete, new work and the craftsman-artist producing many things from a basic core of skills. The pattern of work and the direction of mind are different, as you see if you compare this Pottery with the studio of my old friend the painter and sculptor Jonathan Kingdon. Jonathan is always tackling something new; he can hardly bear to do the same thing twice. I would have got nowhere if I didn't; I'd never have worked out a good glaze, never have found out how to fire lustre, and certainly never have been able to offer anyone a job.

The distinction between the two processes is something I try to hang on to whenever the recurrent debate 'is it art or is it craft?' resurfaces, as it inevitably does many times every year in conferences and periodicals. We are reminded again that every artist is to some extent also a craftsman and that craftsmen are also artists, and some ceramicists get hot under the collar if it is suggested they are not, especially if their prices are high. The usual conclusion is 'Art or craft, what the hell, anyway?' There is, in fact, a real and interesting difference between them.

The two processes 'Many-from-One' and 'One-from-Many' aren't limited to any single field of human activity, nor only to human activity, but reappear in all domains of existence, in the evolution of living forms, in the development of living tissue, as well as in such specifically human fields as economics and politics. The processes exist in the abstract before they take form, and the forms in which they appear, on various and very different scales, all share a cosmic blue-print.

Now I understand better why I was surprised by my evening visit to the workshop. It wasn't the pots themselves. It was the process they belong to, which they share with the leaves on the tree, the pebbles on the seashore, and possibly even the stars in the Christmas sky.

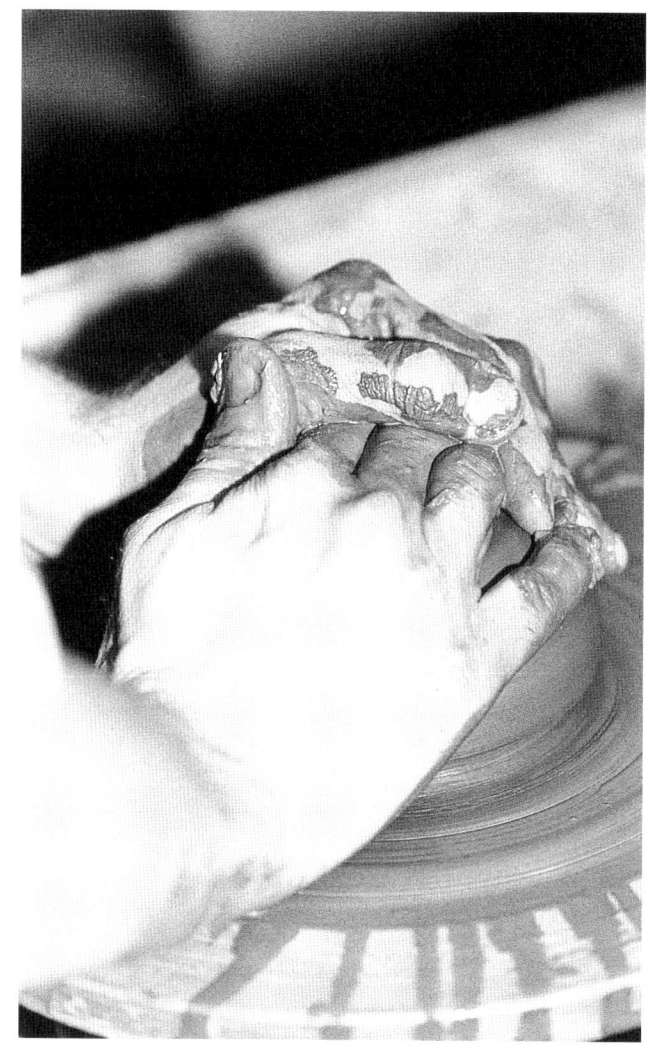

12

AN APPRENTICE

The young man's work turned out to be surprisingly good. The tall forms, textured like antique bronze, looked monumental, although they were actually only fifteen inches high. It was easy to imagine them on a vast scale, in a desert, on a hillside, or against a background of scudding clouds, the jagged edges of the extruded clay silhouetted like a mountain range against the sky. They were complete and convincing far beyond most student work.

Diffidently he reached into the box and took out another bag, carefully untying the cord at the neck. Each piece was kept in a separate bag made of dark blue velvet.

"It was my sister's idea", he said. "It's a good way of keeping things safe. This shape was suggested by one of the stones in the Avenue at Avebury. It made me think of a prophet, someone like Elijah when he listened for God's voice in the wind, only God wasn't actually in the wind after all. I pressed the block to thin it this way and widen it the other side. The way it leans is meant to suggest listening. The texturing is meant to suggest eternity but I'm not sure it really works."

The grainy clay was bedded with some kind of glinting, golden mica where he had scraped down the surface. It reminded me of wind-smoothed stones I had seen in the desert. The idea came through perfectly.

One could see the influence of his teacher, a man I knew quite well. This was natural in someone of Philip's age, but the idea behind the forms was obviously his own. The man and his work were growing on me.

"The last piece doesn't have a bag yet because it's rather big," he remarked as he brought a large wheel-thrown form out of the box. It was a tall, dark container with a narrow base, widening gracefully towards the top and turning slightly inwards at the rim. The upper part had been pressed into an oval and cut to make an undulating edge, which had been finished with irregular twists of extruded clay. I had seen this kind of thing before, but never one as good.

"I brought it to show that I can work on the wheel too, though we didn't do much throwing. They said it only made sense for functional work, which they weren't very keen on. Not that you could call this a functional pot anyway. I thought of it more as a kind of symbol, like another prophet, a man waiting to catch the rain from heaven."

Roger, his teacher, would never have thought like that. He taught brilliantly, but most of his own work was lifeless, like a series of admirable technical exercises. I was glad Philip had managed to hold his own.

And now here he was, hoping to get a job. What should I say? Deciding whether or not to take on a newcomer would be easy if it were simply a matter of assessing his ability. In fact, that is a most unsatisfactory way of reaching a decision. What matters is not how good he is today, but how good he will have become in a year's time. Then how will he take to brushwork and decoration, which he probably hasn't done before? The actual making is only a part of the work, of course: clay and glazes have to be prepared and looked after, kilns packed, wood collected, and so on. How will he get on with all that? And will he play a proper role in selling and dealing with visitors, a vital part of the work which everyone shares? Is he strong, does he smell when he sweats, does he mind the cold? Will he be good company, and how long is he likely to stay? Behind the conversation, the questions go racing through one's mind, and many of them can't be answered or even asked. But what matters most of all is people's response to what is seen around them. If anyone wants body and mind to make our kind of pots, then they will fit in, and sooner or later they will find the necessary skill and resourcefulness.

When someone applies, a sixth sense usually says Yes or No quite early on, and I often prolong the talk simply to make the person feel that he has had a proper hearing. The answer sometimes surprises me but it is usually right. In Philip's case it was clear all along, but I felt responsible for him. Was it really the right thing from his point of view? What would happen to those striking ideas and images of his in a workshop that concentrated on pots for use, decorated with colour and brushwork, almost the opposite of what he had been doing?

There are not many jobs on offer in the world of craft pottery. To find any opening at all is sometimes so tempting that students just coming out of college often fail to see how big the change is going to be. It is easy to suppose that they are going to develop what they have already been doing. In fact, they are virtually making a new beginning. For two or three years they have been encouraged by tutors to develop their individual line, and at the end of the course it is presented with a good deal of flourish in a diploma display . For most people it's a shock to start working and find that the rest of the world isn't very interested.

Philip set my mind at rest. He said that everyone had to adjust if they wanted to try something new. Something familiar always had to be left behind. He was eager to start. I said he must follow his star: if he didn't feel comfortable, he must say so as soon as possible. We agreed he would come for a trial period of three months.

He had beautiful hands, soft but strong, with long, tapering fingers, widening at the tips, and unusually definite joints. Watching him at work you realised what an exquisite instrument the human hand is, and through the hand you felt the intelligence directing it. I never saw him make an inattentive hand-movement. His feet, however, were a different story. He usually wore heavy boots and seldom noticed what he was treading on unless it miaowed.

Though he had not done much work on the wheel he soon became one of the best throwers we ever had. People learn in different ways, basically through either head, heart or hand. Philip learnt by imitating movement, hardly thinking what result he was aiming at. He got the feeling, tried it out, and used his critical faculties afterwards. It was a physical response. His excellent design sense only came into effect later. He said that if a thing doesn't feel right when it's being made, it can't look right when it's finished.

Most of our forms are thrown on the wheel. The weight of clay and the dimensions of each vessel are recorded in our Bible. There are prototypes, but it is not always easy to see differences and follow them, and the final form depends on how the clay is opened out, and the timing. Even simple forms usually need to be introduced by a practical demonstration, and sometimes it takes several days of concentrated effort before a newcomer gets them right.

Philip was a natural. Introducing him to a new form was like a romance, discovering subtleties of profile, balance and texture intuitively understood by us both and bringing them to life. I felt I was simply reminding him of what he knew already, rather than teaching, and he would often exactly foresee a curve or an accent before I could demonstrate it. It was a strange closeness, this meeting through the spinning clay, because in many respects we were very unlike. Through the clay, however, we seemed to be one mind and one body, moved by the same impulses. Of the sixty or so potters I have worked with I have known this only twice. There are many excellent potters with whom nothing like this arises; the forms may be right but the touch is just different. Within the workshop, we can usually tell blindfold which of us has made any particular vessel and potters almost always know their own work just by the feel. Yet with Philip's work and mine neither of us could be sure. It was intriguing, this kinship somehow residing in the molecules of our make-up and experienced through the clay. Occasionally you sense it in the work of an unknown potter dead long ago and far away, and it raises the same wonder as I felt with Philip – "Who are we? Are we really separate individuals? Have we anything of our own?"

Once he had the feel of a form he could repeat it for hours apparently without effort. It is always enjoyable to watch clay taking shape on the wheel, but however often you do it yourself it is quite different seeing it in someone else's hands. Philip worked like a conjuror and before long the boards would be populated with even rows of new pots shimmering with moisture, waiting until they were leather-hard and ready for turning. He could throw large or small equally well, but his touch showed best of all in making handles, when he drew out the snake-like strap of clay between his long forefinger and unusually tipped-back thumb, turning it to soften the edges, firming the join with his fingertips, and sponging it clean. All potters have to be able to do this, but he did it stylishly and without mess.

Philip painted pots with the same flair, with a generous, flowing movement that could be very precise without ever seeming to be careful, instinctively varying the touch and the thickness of the pigment to give lighter or darker colour to the fired glaze. He was best at strong designs with calligraphic brush-strokes, but he could also paint delicate, figurative designs on cups or other small pots when he wished. He could have been a professional cartoonist. Philip's work flowed and danced. He didn't so much do it as allow it to happen. Within eighteen months he had learnt to paint most of our standard designs and was beginning to introduce some excellent figurative themes of his own. But he had a blind spot: like me, he was almost incapable of drawing a straight line.

In other respects, things developed just as they should in a place like this. The ideas and techniques of a co-operative workshop need to be transmissible. It's quite different from the educational process in a college. Initially, at least, people here are learning how to make a specific object, relating their work to clearly defined prototypes or demonstration pieces, going over the process again and again until it is understood and can be repeated. In fact they are doing much more than appearances suggest: they are learning the language of particular brushes, tools and materials rather as one might learn a musical instrument. Learning to make one thing, they are really learning skills that could branch out in many different ways later on. Eventually, having assimilated a variety of different forms and painted designs, they are capable of using them as starting points for their own ideas, for making something new. The freedom to put a new idea to the test is one of the principal differences between a co-operative workshop and a production team. Things are always gently changing. It's not a safe system, but the best results more than make up for the failures and in the long run it is vastly more rewarding..

What did Philip come for? What takes people into pottery? As the world judges it is not a wise move; there's no ladder of promotion to go up, no guarantee of increasing reward, nothing to show without constant effort, a sustained flow of ideas, and a readiness to tackle a succession of unexpected technical problems, yet people are continually being drawn to it from all walks of life. A few are following a strong, creative vision; some have been captivated by the love of clay itself, its magical firmness and pliability. Others, like the extraordinary Bernard Palissy five centuries ago, are enthralled by the transforming effect of fire and heat on clay, glass and colour. Others get into it by reacting against the demands of modern urban life, finding in pottery a platform where they can be independent and self-reliant.

I remembered what Michael Cardew said about this:

> Someone had written about children: 'the world-wide fraternity of children is the greatest of savage tribes and the only one which shows no sign of dying out', and I also reflected that up to a certain age practically all children are good primitive artists.
>
> A child has not got the techniques and the means of expression which we subsequently acquire; but being aware that the world is overflowing with some tremendous significance he has to do something – or rather make something – as a kind of acknowledgement of the mystery. In the West, as children grow older, they have to be educated for a certain kind of civilization and most of them abandon their primeval art-faculty and it never grows beyond the embryonic stage. But some people still insist on discovering for themselves some technical channel through which they can express their wordless inner convictions and communicate them to others in an acceptable, intelligible form – such as pots.[3]

I think these words are true and important, but when I thought about Philip they made me uneasy. By including him in the workshop had I perhaps simply coaxed him into what Cardew would have called 'my kind of civilization' and made him abandon his own line? The work he first showed me had been very different from the things he was so good at making now. What had happened to all those ideas? Thinking about it, I suggested to him that he might do some independent work of his own on the lines of the pieces he showed me when we first met. His reaction was a surprise.

He said he wouldn't want to go back to that now. It was over and done with. They liked you to do sculptural things at the college. That was how they thought, but he was really more interested in making pots. Besides, he liked making things for real people who really wanted them. And he liked meeting people and hearing what they thought.

"In the college we were isolated," he said.

"I asked because I was afraid you were being influenced away from your old ideas."

"Of course I am, and I'm glad of it. That's why I came. You don't have to apologise. Just be yourself. You've got to follow your star too, the same as you told me."

13

EXPORTS

"Export or die" we were continually being told. "Exports are number one priority". It must apply to every country in the world, but in the late 'sixties the government believed that Britain had not yet got the point and it kept reminding us in every possible way. So when a courteous, elderly gentleman asked me, as he signed his cheque, whether I would be interested in exhibiting in Japan, I responded immediately.

"Our people at the Consulate could make contacts for you. That's partly what they are for. Here's my address. Let me know if you'd like to pursue the idea." He didn't mention that he had recently retired after several years as our Ambassador in Tokyo.

The offer was too good to miss. My work had been shown overseas before, but never before in a one-man exhibition. This was a great chance. Besides, exports are number one priority. If the project ended as a classic example of "how-not-to-do-it" it was certainly not the Ambassador's fault.

I had beautiful slides made of some of my best work and despatched them to the Consulate. The people there made contact with Yusuke Aida, a distinguished young Japanese designer who took the project under his wing out of pure kindness. In due course he put me in touch with the Director of the Art Gallery of the Matsuya Store in Tokyo, and after a lengthy and courteous correspondence the exhibition was arranged for March of the following year. Since my work was unknown in Japan the Director regretted that he could not purchase the exhibition outright, but he proposed to take only the minimum commission on sales and to cover the costs of display, printing, and publicity. Yusuke himself volunteered to take personal charge of the presentation.

Some of our friends cautioned that the Japanese had a great deal of pottery already and that it might be like carrying coals to Newcastle, or, as a German friend put it, "like taking owls to Athens". Others reminded me of the immense success of Bernard

Leach's Japanese exhibitions and of the high regard the Japanese had for British ceramics. They pointed out that the greatest discernment exists where an art is already well established and advised me to go ahead.

Most of my personal work over the next eight months was done with the Tokyo exhibition in mind, and from it I selected the best hundred and fifty items. Anders Quistgaard, returning to Denmark after eighteen months in Japan, helped me select those that were in his view the most interesting for Japanese people. We whittled down the final collection to a hundred and twenty pieces, omitting anything we were not entirely sure of. Photographs for advance publicity were sent to the Gallery together with material for the press release.

The Board of Trade and the Customs and Excise people advised us about tariff regulations and documentation and provided a list of recommended shipping agents with good contacts in the Far East. All the work was listed, priced, labelled and packed into boxes lined with wood-wool in five specially made wooden crates capable of withstanding the worst imaginable buffeting. Packing pottery properly is a like an intelligence test in three-dimensional design. The ideal place for each item has to be visualised before making a move. No-one packs pots better than a potter. This consignment received special attention, not only because of the importance of the event but because the premium for insuring pottery against breakage is extremely high, and rather than add that cost to the shipping expenses the work was packed so well that no breakage could possibly occur, only insuring the consignment against total loss. In the event everything arrived at the Gallery in perfect condition and I received a letter in beautiful, honorific English such as only the Japanese can write, expressing their delight at the exhibits and their certainty that the display would call the big attention. Everything was set fair.

Had I known more about Japanese conventions and had more time and money I would have flown to Tokyo for the opening. It is customary in Japan for the artist to be present, and when ceramics are sold in an exhibition a special box is usually made for each piece and the maker is expected to sign the box with a brush in the presence of the buyer. I did not know this and had taken the Gallery Director's expression of deepest regret for my absence as oriental courtesy rather than as a critical commercial warning. Even had I been better informed I would still not have made the journey because of the unexpectedly high cost of dock charges and shipping, on top of which the agents had to pay forty per cent of the value of the goods as import duty before the boxes could be cleared through the port of Yokohama.

EXPORTS

ことば

英国の陶芸家は日本で作品展を開くことに遠慮があります。それは私達が意識しなくても非常に強い東洋からの影響を受けているからであります。
たとえその作風の源がヨーロッパに発しているとしても影響は大きく表われていることでしょう。
私の仕事はヨーロッパ古来からの伝統的な技法を今もってつづけております。それは長い間の陶器愛好家からの要望でもあるからです。
しかし、今回私はじめ協力してくれる友人達の作品展は全く新しい手法による創造的な作品を発表することにいたしました。
この機会にあたりまして是非日本の愛好家の皆様からきびしいご批判を賜わりますようお願申上げます。　　　　　　　　　アレン・ケイガー・スミス

■略　歴　1954〜5　　ロンドン美術工芸専門学校で学ぶ
　　　　　1955　　　　アルダー　マストン　製陶所を創設
　　　　　1957　　　　ロンドン デザイン センターの仕事を引受く
　　　　　1965　　　　英国陶芸作家協会の委員になる
　　　　　1966　　　　ロンドン クラフト センター　審議員になる

Invitation card, 1968. Translated back from Japanese, the message says "There is something reserved for the British studio potters to hold exhibitions in Japan, because we are very strongly influenced by the Orient if it is not conscious. My work has been keeping up the time-honoured tradition of Europe to satisfy the demand of long time lovers. However this time, creative works by myself and my collaborator friends in brand-new technique will be laid before the public..."

Yusuke Aida had asked a representative of the British Council to open the exhibition. This, he said, would give it an official, national status in Japanese eyes. Symbolising the entente, the two national flags would be positioned on either side of the entrance to the Gallery. Unfortunately, to the Director's even deeper regret, the British Council declined the request without explaining why. He sent me a cable explaining his predicament, wondering if there might be some sinister significance in this lack of support. I appealed to the London Office, only to be told that pottery was not art and the Council could not revise its terms of reference. At the eleventh hour Yusuke persuaded a representative of the commercial wing of the Consulate to come. I met him many years later. He had an embarrassing evening. Not only did he know very little about pots and nothing about me, but there were very few people present to hear his speech. Apparently the invitation cards had not been printed in time for the opening and were only circulated three days before the exhibition closed. Since the British Council had already refused to allow Yusuke to refer to their mailing list, the number of invitations distributed cannot have been very large. By the close of the exhibition only five of the exhibits had been sold and the two principal items were purchased by Yusuke himself. When I met him later in England he told me this was not to get me off the hook; he thought they were wonderful.

The remaining hundred and fifteen items had then to be sent back to England. Unfortunately when the representative of the Board of Trade in London had advised me about the tariffs she had omitted to mention a document which, had I forwarded it, would have enabled me to reclaim the import duty. It was now too late and that money was gone for good.

On the bright side, however, I received a telephone call from a gallery in Australia. They had heard about the exhibition and were keen to show any unsold pieces. There was just enough time for the agents to revise the shipping instructions and redirect the boxes to Sydney. Meanwhile, I forwarded an exhibition list to the gallery, together with photographs and another press release. The boxes were still in transit when Sydney telephoned again. Since the exhibition would be arriving from a port outside the Commonwealth Preference Tariff area it would be liable for the maximum import duty on arrival in Australia, amounting to about 43%. This charge, in addition to the freight charges, would lead to unacceptably high prices and the gallery regretted that they now had to withdraw their invitation.

The boxes were therefore disembarked at Sydney and stored intact until my agents could re-consign them back to England. Unfortunately they incurred considerable

EXPORTS

warehouse rental charges before they were re-shipped.

When they eventually reached London the shipping agents telephoned about an unexpected hitch. The British Customs had impounded them. Apparently my personal mark on the base of each piece looked oriental and they suspected the pots might be Far Eastern goods falsely described to evade customs duty, and they were all the more suspicious because the goods had originally been shipped from Yokohama. Before the boxes could be released the Customs and Excise people required proof that the contents were genuinely of British manufacture. I sent them pages from a book of contemporary British potters' marks, but five weeks elapsed before the boxes were cleared. Unfortunately they had incurred warehouse charges while they were waiting and these had to be paid before they were allowed out.

Understandably, I suppose, the shipping agents wanted all outstanding charges to be settled before bringing the boxes back. By this time the costs were considerable: London to Yokohama, plus import duty, and overland to Tokyo; then the return to Yokohama and shipment to Sydney, plus two weeks' warehousing; then from Sydney back to London plus five weeks warehousing, followed by road transport back to Aldermaston. But the problems were not yet quite over.

The exhibition had evidently been hastily re-packed in Tokyo and one could hear things rattling inside the boxes even before the lids were prised off. Unfortunately the Japanese had shipped them uninsured, since they had not been insured on the way out. It had not occurred to me that the Japanese, with their reputation for packaging all kinds of goods, could possibly pack them less well than we had done. As my accountant said, one has to put these things down to experience. More than half the pots were completely broken. I still have one or two things that survived those ill-starred journeys, together with a nice write-up in a Japanese ceramics periodical, and the impressive invitation card as a memorial to the pots that perished.

In the long term it wasn't a total disaster. A year or two later we sold a good many collectors' pots to other Japanese galleries, and when the time came for other overseas exhibitions in New Zealand, Australia, Canada, the U.S.A., Holland, Sweden and elsewhere, I knew things I had not known when I contacted the Consulate in Tokyo keenly aware of the vital importance of exports.

Gold half-noble of Edward III, 1369 (enlarged).

each potter concentrated on two or three lines throughout the year, but it is also clear that this would reduce the satisfaction derived from the work. Only ACS can decide where the balance should lie, but it seems that 50 lines would be a suitable compromise. Lines selling less than £100 a year should be dropped."

(The figures were a surprise and this advice was obviously good sense. We eliminated nearly half the product lines. Those that remained were made better and in larger quantities. To my further surprise, everyone was glad to work for a longer period of time on the same thing instead of having to dodge about. However, in the following years most of the potters still covered a range of about twenty regular products and in the course of time made a number of individual, non-repeat pots as well. No-one would have been happy had their work been restricted as drastically as the report suggested).

"Some product lines are more profitable than others and it is important to know which these are and ensure that they are always in stock. A list of the principal product lines should be drawn up, in order of profitablity, showing the quantity that a potter of average skill can be expected to complete in, say, three days, together with the selling price. Seventeen of the product lines can only be made by the most experienced potters. In these cases the price/time ratio should be considerably higher than for other lines."

(It became clear that three kinds of bowl were the most profitable product and fortunately they were things that we particularly enjoyed making. Once we gave them priority we began to make a good deal more money. The market for these bowls seemed inexhaustible. In order to keep up the supply, several of the surviving product lines were virtually discontinued. It was not difficult to obtain higher prices for things that could only be made by the more experienced potters once the reason was explained).

"Prices. The return on capital is much too low. Only ACS can decide how close he wishes to get to an economic return (which might be over 20%), but it should be higher than 6%. A rough guess is that the selling prices should be increased by about 25% ACS should keep himself informed about prices charged by other craft potteries. Glazing and painting account for around one third of total labour costs: piece for piece Aldermaston ware ought therefore to be priced higher than ware which is not painted or decorated."

(The price increase made no difference to the number of pots we sold. Several customers volunteered that they thought they had been too cheap all along. This was probably true: one of the potters did some market research and discovered that several things we made were cheaper than equivalent ware produced by certain factories. In addition, I introduced the yellow label idea. Regularly made pots that fired particularly well, as they often did in the wood-firings, were marked up by about 25% and were priced with a yellow label. These pots sold just as easily as the rest and the label also helped customers to choose a good piece when they were in doubt).

"Sales. Sales have not hitherto proved any problem: indeed, some shop customers have had to be 'rationed' and other would-be customers refused because of the shortage of stock. At present an average of six transactions a day are handled by the potters, all of whom sell to customers when necessary. This number of transactions can probably be handled without undue disruption of the potters' work, though they are probably one of the causes of the low productivity. The value of sales per person employed is at present much too low. An initial target should be to double the figure, but it should be higher still. Should sales increase, steps should be taken to sell most of the increase through shops and special exhibitions."

(Instead of continuing to ration shop customers, we reduced the trade discount. All the buyers protested and two were never seen again. The others found that the pots were still saleable and continued to buy just as before. We did not try to increase the sales to shops; instead, we reserved a higher proportion of pots for exhibitions. The transactions on the premises inevitably interrupted the flow of the work but they increased the morale: by and large everyone enjoyed meeting people who liked what we made and most customers appreciated being served by a potter rather than a salesperson).

"The workforce. The daily output of a skilled potter producing regularly made product lines is roughly five times greater than that of a trainee and seventeen of the product lines can only be made by skilled potters. Initially, a trainee's work is usually sold at half the normal price. Furthermore, much of the commissioned work and all the exhibition pieces, which have the highest selling prices, can only be made by skilled potters. Thus the value of a skilled potter's output can be estimated as at least ten times that of a trainee. Clearly the proportion of trainees in the workforce is too high, averaging three out of eight. ACS should take steps to find and employ skilled potters rather than select his assistants from enthusiasts who wish to learn how it is done".

(The moment this was put into effect the benefits began to show. From now on, with one exception, I only employed people with some experience. Even so, they always needed further training, especially in decorating).

"Wages. The wages of a competent potter after two years' training are only 1.5

times higher than those of a beginner, and the wages of a skilled potter are only about three times higher. Again, this shows the importance of limiting the number of trainees."

(Every trainee was paid enough to live on even though their output seldom covered their wages for the first nine months. Alternatively, one could have charged an apprenticeship premium or offered no wages at all during the early training period, but this would have ruled out some worthwhile people. The differential between skilled potters and trainees was increased by offering overtime piecework to the more skilled people and by graduated bonus payments at the end of the year).

"Supervision. At present almost all supervision of the work is done by ACS. Training beginners and checking the quality of the finished ware occupies 20-25% of ACS's time. As in many other activities, one man can seldom supervise carefully the work of more than six to eight others. Another person should undertake part of the work of supervision. It is a commonplace in industry that the best craftsmen do not always make the best foremen. If the person chosen is not a success as a supervisor, ability to supervise should be one of the criteria in selecting new potters."

(This was more or less solved by appointing another person to help with supervision, though it continued to take quite a lot of my own time. Whenever possible the supervisory work was extended to other members of the team who had sufficient experience. On the whole this worked quite well: passing on what one has recently learnt is one of the best ways of consolidating it for oneself).

"Numbers. Space is the main factor determining the number who can be employed, which appears to be ten, including ACS himself. Assuming that part of the supervision can be undertaken by another person, and if the proportion of skilled potters can be increased to eight out of ten, it should be possible to double the sales turnover within a year and to achieve a considerably higher figure in the years following. The existing accommodation can house two married and about six unmarried employees. If any further cottages in or near the village become vacant it would be wise to buy them even if it involved using borrowed money."

(This was not followed up).

"Division of labour. Most large businesses operate on the principles of specialisation and division of labour. In a commercial pottery, a thrower, a caster, a mouldmaker and a decorator seldom know how to do more than their own job. At Aldermaston the employees are trained to do all the jobs. They probably achieve greater satisfaction in this way, but partly as a result output per person is very low and would probably rise if there were greater specialisation. This is an important dividing line between a craft business and a business run primarily for profit."

(A crucial point. It was not followed up. The reasons are explained later).

"Cost of materials. In 1973 the cost of materials jumped from an average of 8.4% over the previous ten years to 15.2% and is likely to increase further with inflation. Thus while materials have hitherto been a relatively small item they are now of the same order of importance as overheads and greater time spent on control of expenditure would be justified. More attention should be given to competitive quotations and alternative suppliers, increased attention to control of wastage and possible substitution of cheaper for more expensive materials. Three items, glaze frits, clay and tin oxide at present account for about 54% of the expenditure. In most businesses, however, it is seldom that one big saving can be achieved: the best results are normally achieved through a number of small savings."

(Very helpful advice. By applying direct to manufacturers of tin oxide we were able to buy it for 25% less. Also, the price of standard glaze frits and other materials varied considerably from one supplier to another and about 20% could often be saved by dealing through the less well known firms).

"Overheads. Over a period when the overheads of most businesses have increased greatly, it is striking to find that they have remained more or less steady. This may be partly due to ACS's habit of doing most of his own office work instead of employing a part-time secretary/typist, which would be preferable, allowing more freedom for other responsibilities, and time given by AMCS to repairs, maintenance, deliveries to galleries, etc. In the long run, and especially if sales increase, this extra work may not be sustainable. Overheads are likely to increase and provision should be made for this."

(I bought a calculator, a dictating machine and a small photocopier, which saved a great deal of time. Initially the letters were done by a part-time typist and later by one of the potters. Most of the girls who worked for me were in fact competent typists but they kept quiet about it until the situation became critical. Eventually, part-time secretarial work became a condition of employment for one of the girls. Wages and book-keeping were always kept separate and were done by a part-time person from outside).

"Budgetting. Consideration should be given to the preparation of forward budgets and to their revision and comparison with actual results at half-yearly intervals."

(This was done on an annual basis, though less systematically than was advised. Its full importance only became apparent when we accepted the commission for the very large lustre pots (Chapter 18) which could not have been done without preparing a detailed forward budget)."

"Management accounting. Financial accounts do not seem to be sufficiently used as a basis for management accounting and control. Some management ratios have been worked out and these should be extended and kept up to date in future. For them to be of greatest use:

1. trends over a period should be examined.
2. the accountants should prepare draft accounts more quickly and
3. preparation of half-yearly accounts should be considered in times of rapid inflationary change.

Basic management ratios averaged over the past six years, were as follows, the figures being % of sales and finished stock.

Consumption of materials	10.4
Electricity	2.2
Wages and national insurance	43.2
Overheads	18.8
Net profit	25.4

(This advice was followed up regularly. The trends shown by the management ratios provided vital information about what was happening and also gave a sound basis for assessessing the level of wages and bonuses).

The report included the following far-sighted comments. "The application to craftsmen of normal business indices of success, such as return on capital employed, production and sales per person employed, rate of growth, can only be done after trying to see whether the pursuit of such indices would destroy what they themselves most value. In the case of some individuals this would probably happen and, save in a few cases (say silverware and jewellery), this is likely to place a low limit on their net income — a limit of which they are generally aware and accept.

Some, on the other hand, have a wife and family and aim at a rather higher standard of living which they can only achieve by employing assistants. There are few activities in which one person can supervise more than about half a dozen others and this, again, places a limit on the size of a 'one-man business' (as distinct from an individual working more or less on his own).

If a craftsman wishes to expand his activities beyond this point he is almost bound to have to learn something about running a business, as well as maintaining his own characteristic style and the quality of his goods. Expansion of businesses big or small is all too often carried through at the expense of quality."

I did what I could to follow up Oliver's suggestions, with two deliberate exceptions. I did not attempt to increase our numbers to ten. We had been there before and it posed considerable difficulties. A subtle change came about as soon as the numbers passed eight: the general spirit of supportive accord was lost and I was no longer in close touch with each person. As a result some troublesome events took place and I did not wish to risk it again. Secondly, I did not try to introduce specialisation of labour, even though this would almost certainly have made the business more profitable. I felt that whatever profit it produced would be at the expense of something even more valuable, the all-round, direct experience of the transformation of material and the growth of each person's creative imagination and self-reliance. It is arguable that the numerous exhibitions we held in the years ahead, consisting essentially of unique, individual pieces, would not have been possible had each person's job been made more specialised.

We might have made more money had I followed the advice on this important point, but the fact that no fewer than thirty-six of the potters eventually established successful studio-workshops of their own, each with its own distinct style and character, confirmed my belief that this was the better course. This was one of those 'things most valued' which Oliver recognised as being sometimes more important than the indices of business success.

Happily, the benefits brought by following up the other sections of the report began to appear almost immediately and enabled us to continue working for the next twenty years relatively prosperously and without finding ourselves at the cliff edge again. I should have appreciated, years before, the important points that Oliver clarified for us, but he assured me, characteristically, that it is not unknown for larger and more sophisticated businesses to get into similar difficulties for much the same reasons.

15

THE FACTORY

At long last the Canadian order was completed and packed for transit. The four crates were duly collected by the shipping agents and consigned to Georg Jensen Toronto. We brought out the champagne. The consignment was a large one by our standards and in due course we were rewarded with several thousands of pounds, a considerable sum in the early 'seventies. It had been a craftsmanlike job, requiring steady repetition and constant attention to detail; craftsmanlike in the old sense of the word, meaning that it was done to a precise specification and every item was consistent and attentively made by hand: lidded soup bowls, dessert bowls, small covered tureens, plates, coffee cups and saucers, coffee jugs, milk pots, sugar bowls and serving dishes, all painted in a deep blue-green and, for the most part, fired in the wood kiln, which makes the colour especially rich and luminous.

This kind of order is not a quick way to get rich. Every lid and saucer must fit, every bowl and plate must match and stack. The pots have a job to do and whatever artistic quality they have is a secondary consideration. Nevertheless it is highly satisfying, provided you don't have to maintain the discipline for ever and ever. Everyone looks forward to some relatively relaxed and free work after completing a consignment of this kind.

About a month later a letter arrived from Canada. Apparently almost all the pots had been sold in three days and the store required more of the same. They wanted twenty times more within three months, for Christmas. Next year they would require a quarter of a million pounds worth, followed by equal or greater consignments for the following five years.

The initial requirement took us totally by surprise. Even if more time had been allowed I simply could not have asked the potters to produce it. As for the enormous

THE FACTORY

follow-up, it was beyond possibility. However willing, the potters needed variety. We were not machines and beyond a certain point people cannot be programmed. I had to write explaining that the order was beyond our capacity. A week later came a telephone call from Mr Zimkowsky, the President of the Company. What was the real problem? he asked. There was a serious demand. Does one fly in the face of demand? My explanations were not agreeable; he would be in England next month and would visit.

A few weeks later, a jovial man of about sixty, in a dark winter coat and wearing a round Russian lambswool hat, leaned over the stable door that opens into the workshop and asked for the director. I washed the clay from my hands and introduced myself. Mr Zimkowsky entered and looked around with obvious amusement. His Canadian speech was spiced with a powerful Russian accent.

"So this is the place. Problem is abundantly clear!"

He walked in further, towards the wheels where Edgar, David and Juliet were throwing and surveyed the scene The he turned to me and laughed, deep-throated Russian laughter. He grasped my hand.

"Problem is well understood. My friend, you and I are going to start a factory! We take lunch together and discuss. My car is outside."

I could see the chauffeur idly surveying the pots in our window. The only restaurant appropriate to the situation was some four miles away. My clothes were utterly unsuitable and I was apprehensive about the size of the bill, but it had to be done. Fortunately, Zimkowsky insisted on paying.

He said we must first consider the product, secondly the manufacturing requirements and thirdly, the raising of capital and our financial agreement. If we got the first two right the third consideration would be no problem. As far as the product was concerned, he said, the potential market should not be underestimated: the company had several subsidiaries in North America. The merchandise would be sold in Toronto and widely distributed elsewhere. Moreover, as I must know, the parent Georg Jensen company was Danish and we must bear in mind the likelihood of European outlets in the future. The tableware should be available in three alternative colours, a sea-colour, which we had already, a desert colour and a spring colour. "So far as concerns market, this is the psychology of colour." Naturally, the range would need to be extended: more oven-to-table items, vessels for condiments and sauces, for salads and dessert, tea cups and saucers and teapots, candlesticks...

The factory should be located in the United Kingdom, as I must be in closest possible contact with it. Besides, this could be important in following up the European potential. Initially we would not think too big: a workforce of about thirty persons should be sufficient. Ideally an entirely new factory would be desirable, but in practice it would be preferable to purchase an existing business with equipment and a basic labour force already on the site. Such businesses were not hard to find with the help of an intelligent agent. He appreciated, of course, that technical expertise would be required to translate the hand-painted designs into an industrial product, but in Stoke-on-Trent "under-employed and under-rewarded technical knowhow is abundant". So much for the general plan. From London he would initiate the enquiries about factory premises and we would meet and discuss further.

By the time the car dropped me off back at the Pottery the prospects, and perhaps the excellent Chardonnay, had gone slightly to my head. Everything had happened so fast; it was difficult to recognise that this workshop with its clay-splattered potters was where the whole idea had started. Now, I couldn't help seeing it through Zimkowsky's eyes. Everything was so small, so basic, so informal. North America, Denmark, Europe? Perhaps the whole scheme was a fantasy.

Yet it was in line with something that had been in my mind for several years. A recurrent question in a small workshop is what to do about the best sellers. Certain things sold extremely easily, especially our lidded casserole dishes and some of our jugs, jars, bowls and plates. Everyone liked making these things but they were enjoyable partly because the work alternated between them and a variety of relatively freely made pots that sold in smaller numbers. If one concentrated on the limited range of pots most in demand the work would be much less fun. People might earn more, but the morale would decline because this was not really what they had come for. As Edward Lucie Smith wrote a year or two later, "the whole method of operation involves a constant if subdued conflict between what is good for the business and what is good for the individual."[4] This had slightly disturbed me for some time. In practice, therefore, I did not attempt to follow up the demand for our best sellers and sometimes they were discontinued before people could get fed up. If, however, one could collaborate with a factory, converting certain designs into something that could be manufactured industrially, the royalties would allow us to follow up other ideas back at home with a kind of financial life-raft beneath us. I had tried to make contact with factories through the Design Centre but nothing had come of it, understandably perhaps, because I am not a trained industrial designer. I had no credentials to offer, only products.

THE FACTORY

Here, now, was Mr Zimkowsky, President of of Georg Jensen, Canada, wanting to do exactly what I had been hoping for.

"It's an incredible breakthrough," I told Anne-Marie.

"Maybe", she said, "but not quite yet."

We held numerous further discussions at the Zimkowskys' London flat, accompanied by delicate luncheons provided by his manservant. We met his sales director, property agents, distributors, a copyright lawyer and technical experts who discussed the conversion of the prototypes into an industrial equivalent. Everything seemed wonderfully positive. Then one day Zimkowsky telephoned to say that a possible site had come up in Stoke-on-Trent and we must inspect it. I was finishing an important commission at the time but it had to wait. The opportunity was too good to miss. We met the agent in Stoke a few days later.

Property agents' prospectuses are not always scrupulously accurate but we were unprepared for the vastness and extreme dilapidation of the bleak Victorian factory building he showed us, with its perforated roof, dripping walls, its antique and rust covered machinery. It must have been decaying for generations. The agent was unabashed. There was a smaller, more modern unit not far away, available at a very reasonable price. This turned out to be three Nissen huts, the damp floors laminated with old commercial documents, and with no furnishings other than a broken air compressor and a filter press with a cracked frame. Again the agent remained resolute, saying that a number of other properties were about to come on to the market and he would keep in touch. The journey had been a total waste of time and the whole environment was unutterably depressing, including the dismal pub where we lunched. None of this seemed to bother Zimkowsky. He said it was necessary to investigate the market and a few false trails were only to be expected.

I got back home late that night and Anne-Marie asked how things had gone. "Isn't it incredible," I said, "incredible that an agent could possibly get it so wrong."

"Disappointing, yes, but not incredible."

Meanwhile, there were further working luncheons at the flat in London, mainly concerned with the scope of the range of tableware and anticpated changes in consumer demand. On one of these occasions I was introduced to Zimkowsky's London deputy, a younger man, agreeable enough, but with none of his leader's verve. These meetings were enjoyable and seemed to provide some insight into how business really works, but it was costing a lot in travel and above all in time. Every luncheon meant a considerable amount of uncompleted personal work back in the Pottery and it was beginning to pile up. Eventually I felt obliged to ask if the Georg Jensen Company would cover my expenses and pay a fee for the time devoted to these consultations. Zimkowsky said he completely understood the problem.

"But my friend," he said, "from this enterprise you and I are going to make SO MUCH MONEY that such anxieties can forthwith be dismissed."

Our next expedition was to a site in the West of England. It looked highly suitable to me but Zimkowsy said we should not rush into a decision. He had confidentially learned recently of a factory in Scotland whose owners were keen to sell as a going concern. This might be exactly what we were looking for. Meanwhile, patience was of the essence.

A week later he once again asked me to a working luncheon with his deputy. he explained that he had to return to Canada. His deputy knew all about our plans and would press ahead as soon as opportunities arose and would keep in touch.

He didn't. When I telephoned him a few weeks later to ask if any further news had come from the factory in Scotland he said there had been developments but not yet far enough advanced to justify a visit. Later he reported that the owners still wished to sell but that some clarification was needed from Toronto before action could be taken. Later again I was told that, unfortunately the owners had pre-empted us and concluded a sale elsewhere. The deputy never got in touch again. Next time I rang up he was abroad. After that he vanished into thin air.

I liked Zimkowsky and trusted him. I think he was serious about the project and it could have worked, but he had other fish to fry and he was a long way away. I could have tried to pursue the idea on my own, but it involved terrifying liabilities in money and time and I would have been quite out of my depth. Rightly or wrongly, I felt that to persevere with this scheme would deprive the Pottery of the attention it constantly needed and put everything we had done there at risk. Anne-Marie had seen it all along.

An association with an industrial producer could have made good sense for us and for the factory concerned, and I still believe that a number of small workshops have a design and idea potential that industry could and should follow up. It has happened in other European countries but only to a relatively small extent in the United Kingdom. The Council of Industrial Design recognised the possibilities and one of its departments was supposed to encourage them. A number of craftsmen like myself were keen to participate and regularly exhibited products in the Design Centre but there was virtually no response from the industry and very little happened.

THE FACTORY

In the next few years we did in fact have serious discussions about designs for industrial manufacture with three factories, two large ones and one small. In each case I made a number of prototypes but the small factory was the only one to follow them up. We produced a range of decorated tableware and ovenware and a few new items based on my prototypes. From my point of view this was only a half-way stage. Most of the existing shapes seemed to me unsatisfactory and ideally the whole range should have been re-designed, not simply one or two pieces. However, this would have involved considerable expense and a major hiccup in production and the owners of the factory were not willing to take the risk. They also found that their British retailers were not sufficiently up-market and the new designs did not fit their price range. Everything we produced was in fact sold in Barcelona. I found this encouraging, but the sales manager did not take the same view. He called it the cuckoo in the nest.

After about eighteen months the production stopped. The royalties had been adequate, but it was no heartbreak when the project came to an end. At last we were able to attend wholeheartedly to our own production and in the long run that was what counted most. We had lustre to fire and exhibitions to prepare for; it was time to switch into another way of thinking. If in the future any association with a factory were to arise, the initiative must come from them. For the time being I had done enough running around.

POTTERY, PEOPLE AND TIME

Top: The Mocking.
Bottom: "...the veil of the Temple was rent in twain and the earth did quake...".

16

STATIONS OF THE CROSS

The project developed out of an attempt to escape from my own habits. Having worked on the same themes for some time, I was beginning to feel stale. One day a completely different idea came up and I sketched it out on a large, shallow dish. The initial idea was vague, but it resolved itself into two enigmatic figures in conversation, and behind them a boy kicking a ball and several other figures in energetic movement. The freely drawn composition left plenty of scope for imaginative interpretation.

The piece fired well and was displayed it in our gallery across the road. There it remained for about a year, almost forgotten.

As I was painting in the rear workshop one afternoon there appeared behind me a man of about my own age in the black robe and heavy shoes of a Benedictine monk. He was holding the dish. He said it was exactly what the Abbey wanted as a gift of thanks for the architect who had recently completed a new parish church for them at Burghfield, a few miles away.

It is always reassuring when someone responds to a new idea, and I was pleased to have made a sale to this courteous man. As soon as he had gone, the plate grew in my estimation and I thought of making other versions. Events intervened, however, and the dish with the figures, like many other things in an active workshop, passed right out of mind.

Later in the year the monk, Father Leonard Vickers O.S.B., reappeared.

"The Visitation was a great success," he said. "Our architect was delighted, and we both hope you will consider a new project, perhaps rather an unusual one."

New projects proposed by disarmingly courteous people often mean long drawn-out discussions leading to nothing, so I was wary. I wondered, besides, what he meant by the Visitation. Could this be a Roman Catholic term for a monastic inspection, or a special event like the arrival of a cardinal?

"Don't you remember the dish?" he asked, "the one with Our Lady and her cousin Elizabeth and the boy with a football, and the other figures?"

I had never thought of it as the Visitation. I tried to remember the composition more clearly.

"Yes. The two principal figures could be read that way. It would make sense, but what about the others?"

"They signify the continuity of everday life, which goes on just the same while an important spiritual event is taking place. Isn't that how you intended them?"

I wished now that I had. He continued,

"Then perhaps the subconscious will prove equally effective for our new project. We need a set of Stations of the Cross for St. Oswald's. The traditional ones have become clichés and the modern ones are too stark. People need a key, a proper image, to lead them into the subject. You could do it for us, you know, if you wanted to."

I hesitated.

"It's quite clear from the Visitation dish," he continued.

"But I wasn't even thinking about the Visitation'.

"Perhaps that's why it's so unusual. You might be able to do the Stations of the Cross too, without even thinking about them. But seriously, do please consider it. I know you can do it. There's plenty of time."

I promised to think it over. I felt extremely unsure about doing it, but I would have liked to be able to.

Several months passed and from time to time I remembered this vague commitment, first simply as a possibility, then as a nagging burden. Nothing had been promised, but sooner or later a decision had to be made.

The feeling of the series as a whole was quite clear. I wanted it to convey the historical Passion, an actual trial and execution taking place in time, and also the Passion as a perpetually re-enacted drama, concerning all places and all times, past, present and to come. The Cross was to be a real cross of torment, but also a symbol of the meeting of the eternal, the vertical, with time, the horizontal. It would appear as a cross of wood and as a cross of light, both at once, as in the mystical Hymn of Jesus. On Father Leonard's suggestion the green background was also to be patterned with small crosses, signifying mankind as witnesses of the Passion. All human beings, he said, have in their innermost hearts the cross of light, and all have to share, one way or another, in the cross of wood.

STATIONS OF THE CROSS

But how to begin? I wasn't even sure exactly what subjects the Stations of the Cross consist of. And if possible I wanted to work without referring to any existing versions of the subjects, ancient or modern. Then the technicalities had to be considered: Father Leonard had suggested mural tiles, but a visit to the little church, with its modern wood construction and its open, light interior showed immediately that tiles would be wrong. It would be better to use concave dishes, for which we already had a mould. They could be made with tapering fins at the back, to tilt them forward, and attached to brackets on the wall by means of rods slotted through holes in the fins. The edges would be painted with a red border pattern to relate them to the painted crucifix.

As for the drawings, since 'Jesus falls' comes three times in the traditional sequence, it seemed best to begin with that subject. Various members of the family were persuaded to pose, draped in sheets, carrying a fence post with one arm and supporting themselves on the sitting room floor with the other. After several sessions I had a sheaf of sketches in charcoal, pencil and ink-brushwork, all totally unacceptable, like crude reminiscences of a bible picture book. Then I tried working from how it felt rather than what it looked like, and took up the position of Jesus myself. This got nearer to the essentials of the subject, without the distraction of literal details, but any kind of working drawing was still a mile away.

I had started this exercise in privacy at home, but it caught up with me in the Pottery. While working on something else I would suddenly get a new idea about the angle of the body and adopt the position in the back workshop.

"What the hell's going on?" shouted Jason, finding me spread-eagled on the floor.

"He's trying to do Jesus falling for the third time".

"God help us", said Jason.

Things weren't going too well. Unless something developed soon, I would have to decline the commission. I kept putting off the decision, not wishing to disappoint Father Leonard, nor to miss something I wanted to be able to do.

Perhaps as a result of taking up the poses myself, an idea came to me one evening by the fireside. I saw that so far I had been trying to draw from the outside, like an illustrator in front of a theatrical scene, concentrating on what it looks like, rather than trying to get inside the subject and discover its meaning. Gazing into the embers, I suddenly saw in my mind's eye St. Peter warming his hands at the brazier in the high-priest's courtyard, caught by the serving-girl's accusation, "This man also was with him". Peter denies it three times and then the cock crows. The scene composed itself as lines of force, Peter in the direct line between Jesus and the girl; the girl staring at Peter, and Jesus watching them both. The cock was perched on a cone in the centre background and Peter was caught between all three, wishing the ground would swallow him up.

It was all so clear I could draw the lines of force and the figures without hesitation. Almost immediately, another subject took shape, also as lines of force. This time it was the pointing hands of the accusers homing in on the central figure of Jesus in the Condemnation, with Jesus standing firm in total self-possession. This subject led into other lines of force in the Mocking, the upright figure of Jesus, head bowed, surrounded by the gesticulations of the tormentors in a crazy dance. In a similar way the Agony in the Garden and the Last Supper also took form, so that by two in the morning five subjects had more or less sketched themselves in a manner I was sure was basically right, although a lot more work needed to be done on it.

Within a few days the sketches for the Crucifixion, the Death on the Cross, and the Entombment followed in much the same way. By the time Father Leonard came to look at them, only two subjects were missing. I never managed to 'see' those two subjects, though they were of course included in the series.

I asked him if the Last Supper came into the traditional series. And what about the Agony in the Garden? I had an uneasy feeling that they did not, but I would have liked to include them.

"We needn't be bound by precedents," he said. "There's no need to show Jesus falling three times. One image is enough, and that leaves room for two others. I've always felt the Last Supper should be included, and I assumed you'd want to include the Garden. You could make other changes too if you wish. I knew all along you could do it."

Within a few weeks the first dishes had been biscuit-fired and were ready for glazing and painting. I had hoped to work on the whole set without interruption but this was impractical. It was slow work and there were many other things to be done. Each subject involved a certain emotional commitment and I could not proceed from one to the next without a break. I didn't follow the numerical sequence but simply started on which ever subject became clear in my mind's eye.

Slowly, slowly the group of completed images was growing, but about half the way through I began to wonder if they would ever be finished. Each one took far longer than expected and I was seldom uninterrupted for more than fifteen minutes by queries about current work, telephone calls and visitors. Amongst them came six people from the Burghfield parish asking to see how the work was getting on. Their response was enormously encouraging. The shortcomings seemed to evaporate in their presence, and they fully understood the idea behind each composition. During the next three months other small groups came from the parish, and their enthusiasm helped me to complete the subjects I was least sure of.

At last the whole set was completed, or so I supposed until Father Leonard himself came to look at it.

"Since we have disregarded convention", he said, "I'd like to suggest adding a fifteenth subject, the Resurrection. Perhaps you could do it in your golden-red lustre? I've never seen it included in the series, but it should be."

I was slightly thrown by this suggestion, feeling like a runner who finds that the finishing-line has suddenly been moved on, but the idea made sense and I just hoped once again to 'see' the composition in time to complete it for Easter. Again the lines of force came to my aid. In the last of the original fourteen subjects, the Entombment, the body of Jesus lay within the semi-circular arch of the entrance to the tomb, attended by two kneeling figures silhouetted against the light beyond. In the Resurrection dish the semi-circular entrance was seen from outside, as a dark shape, forming the centre of the composition. In front of it was the light, vertical figure of the risen Christ, staff in hand, and at his feet the curved contours of sprawling soldiers sleeping.

This subject had to be consigned to the uncertainties of the lustre kiln, itself entered through a semi-circular vault. It emerged golden-red and shining. The fifteen images were finally installed in the church a few days before Holy Week.

I cannot feel that my series of the Stations of the Cross is altogether successful as a work of art, not that its validity depends entirely on that consideration. Part of the point of an open workshop like ours is to be able to respond to other people's ideas. By responding, one often lands in unfamiliar territory. It is a weakness and a strength at one and the same time. This important commission was more unfamiliar than most and it would have been easier in a medium which permits alterations, instead of on a ceramic glaze where second thoughts are almost impossible. Even with much more skill and experience, it would still have been difficult to respond adequately to a theme of this magnitude. However, what I did is sincere and it serves its purpose in being 'readable' by many different kinds of people as they celebrate Passiontide and Easter year by year. I gave this work all I had to offer at the time and was rewarded beyond measure by the response of the people of the parish.

Two years later Leonard Vickers went to the U.S.A., where he later became Abbot of St. Anselm's Abbey, Washington D.C. He returned to England in 1989, having been elected eighth Abbot of Douai in Berkshire. He died unexpectedly only nine months later on September 3rd 1990, a man of rare quality, greatly loved.

17

A PARTY

A letter arrived a few days ago from Anne, who used to work with me in the 'sixties and is now in America. She and her husband recently attended a dinner at the British Embassy in Washington. Almost the first thing she saw was the pair of large lustre jars which we were commissioned to make a few years ago. Apparently they have been moved from the first floor to a more honourable position and now stand on either side of the staircase.

This is a happy ending after all our troubles. The work on these very big pots, about forty-five inches high, took us the best part of a year and to get the two we actually had to make nine. They were commissioned by the Property Services Agency, which maintains and furnishes various kinds of national property, from army barracks to embassies. In the old days ambassadors were expected to furnish the embassies themselves, and it was assumed that their grand homes already contained enough silver and glass, paintings, hangings and statues etc. to equip the establishment in the required style. Nowadays the State provides most of it by buying from the antique market, but prices have risen steeply in the last few years and apparently it is now cheaper to buy from the living than from the dead. So contemporary artists and craftsmen come into the scene, though not exactly for the reasons we might have wished.

Each jar was handbuilt from coils of clay on a turntable. It was slow work; the coils have to be carefully smoothed together as the vessel grows, and one has to allow time for the lower part to stiffen before adding the weight of more clay further up, otherwise they go out of shape. It is particularly difficult to control the clay as the form widens; the slightest irregularity tends to increase as the form extends upwards and outwards.

One of the beauties of the coiling method is that even if the form is basically symmetrical it is softened by the method of construction and the symmetry is never precise. A coiled vessel always feels different from a thrown one and the profile can be extremely subtle. Potters who regularly make coiled forms can work fast and with complete assurance and it is no accident that the best coil-pots come from warm, dry climates in which the clay stiffens rapidly as the form expands, making it easier to control. Some of the finest coiled pots ever made are amongst the most ancient, such as the neolithic funerary jars from Kansu in north west China. In the presence of vessels such as these one stands in awe. The forms radiate the inner silence.

Be that as it may, one has to start from where one is. We had not made many coiled forms before, and none of them approached the size required for this commission. Besides, our climate is by no means warm and dry, so we were not surprised to encounter a few problems.

The first jar warped so much as it dried that we didn't bother to fire it. The next two blew out their bases in the biscuit-firing: they had been dried a long time, but evidently not long enough. They should have been placed on a perforated stand, or on their sides, so that the base could dry from underneath. The next two survived but the shapes were not good enough for the embassy. They were eventually fired successfully with lustre and were sold privately, acknowledging them as trial pieces. Numbers six and seven were very good shapes and survived the biscuit-firing perfectly. They needed two further firings, one for the glaze and one for the lustre.

Meanwhile there was a twenty-first birthday to celebrate. The new workshop was cleared for the occasion. Rugs and kelims were hung over the storage shelves, a help-yourself buffet supper was spread out in the throwing-room, and the packing area became the bar. It was pleasing to see so many of our larger ceremonial bowls, platters and jugs coming into their own for displaying the food and drink, and most of the plates and bowls in the showroom were used for serving it out. Amplifiers for the music were installed near the kiln and mats were spread on the floor for a singer and a guitar player. Apart from one or two racks of pots, and bottles of white wine and champagne on ice in the sink, the place could have been mistaken for a night-club with ethnic overtones. For the finishing touches, leafy branches were arranged in the angles of the roof, vases of flowers were placed between the candles along the windows, and the two big jars were placed opposite each other on each side of the dance-floor.

There must have been between forty and fifty guests altogether, about as many as

A PARTY

there was room for. The evening started with a something of a surprise. At the bottom of our invitation it said "Dress: funky". We weren't sure what Jason meant by this but we did our best, and arrived at the party feeling slightly unsure of ourselves. We were taken aback when the first people we met were Jason's parents, immaculately turned out, Keith in tails and Jacq in a long evening dress. They were looking uneasy too. Behind them we could see an animated assembly dressed in an extraordinary assortment of clothing, completely unexpected except by the two people who sent out the invitations. At the bottom of each card they had written 'Dress' followed by different instructions for each group of guests. One card said 'Dress Formal', another, 'Dress Exotic', others said 'Funky', 'Oriental', 'As you are', 'Sporty', 'Academic', and one invitation, sent to an ex-girlfriend, said 'Nothing'. She responded bravely, arriving barefoot in the shortest ever see-through nightie.

Some people were already dancing when Anne-Marie and I arrived, others jostling for drinks or supper around the converted work-benches, and here and there were groups of people on rugs, chatting or tuning musical instruments. The familiar clay-smell blended with alcoholic vapours from the bottles we had all contributed, the usual colourful assortment from unheard of vineyards. The company included all ages from ten to seventy. It was style without formality.

A good time was had by all, a very good time indeed. Like most of the older guests, Anne-Marie and I went home when the party began to thin out around one o' clock but it went on for several hours more. We heard about it next day.

Apparently it became livelier, reaching a peak around three in the morning when Katinka appeared with a caponising knife, having drunk a good deal of vodka. She shouted that certain people were going to get castrated. It was a small instrument, extremely sharp. They tried to wrest it from her. Several candles were extinguished in the scuffle and Katinka was finally waylaid in semi-darkness. As the caponising knife was retrieved the big jar beside her crashed to the ground.

It was unfortunate, but a twenty-first is a one-off and there was no point in spoiling it for what couldn't be undone. Some people felt the real party was only just beginning. The dancing grew wilder. There was a sound of breaking glass and some plates fell. A voice began intoning 'Happy Birthday'. "That was yesterday," someone shouted, "shut him up". In the melée the second jar went over and broke into pieces on the concrete floor.

I received anguished apologies the next day, together with a promise that replacement pots would be made, as good as those that were lost, or better. The new

A PARTY

pots were in fact much better than the originals. However hard one tries, first attempts are seldom right through and through, and the larger the scale the more difficult it is. Doing it over and over again, the details begin to come together, the consistency of the clay, the timing, the pressure of the hand. The scale of the form becomes physically familiar and one get a clearer sense of the object as a whole. The confidence shows. One feels this assured presence in hand-built pots from communities where people make them all the time and live with them. To reach it, there are no short cuts.

We were only in the early stages, but the repetitions forced upon us by the accident were beginning to take effect. By the time the ninth pot of the series was completed it was hard to recall why the first ones had been difficult and taken so long. Eventually the replacements were all fired successfully and the two required for the commission were duly delivered to the P.S.A. and shipped to Washington. Perhaps it was foolish to allow the original jars to be used to add tone to the party, but it turned out for the best. Without the experience of making these large vessels several times over we would never have dared undertake a much larger commission that came our way some years later, the 'Big Pots' project described in the next chapter.

18

BIG POTS

This is the most challenging project we have ever taken on, and the longest. It's too big a job for a studio and too unpredictable for a factory. I think it could only be tackled by a group of potters working closely together as a team, like us. Even now we are surprised to find ourselves in midstream, the more so because we got there almost by accident.

It all began with a general enquiry from the architects Chapman Taylor Partners. They sent the same open letter to a number of people and I've no idea how many replies they received. Probably not many, because what they wanted was several dozen pots four or five feet high for the new headquarters of the Pearl Assurance Company at Lynch Wood, near Peterborough.

I responded more to clear my correspondence file than with any serious idea of getting involved, sending them colour prints of the largest pots we had previously made, and explaining that the size and the quantity posed considerable problems. Amongst the photographs were several large lustre pots, including the two big vases made for the British Embassy in Washington.

Nothing might ever have happened but for Julian's new photographic enlarger. To demonstrate what it could do he produced not the standard size I asked him for, but some enormous, highly-coloured prints, so big that it was hard to find an envelope to post them in. I expected to hear no more of the matter, pleased that at least I had not simply shelved the enquiry.

I had forgotten all about it when, months later, the architects telephoned to arrange a date to discuss the idea further. Evidently only a few people had responded. Having answered their enquiry I could hardly put them off, but fortunately they were very busy and could only come six weeks later, which gave me time to think. The only possible way of following up their ideas seemed to be by making prototypes and drawings of the big pots and subcontracting the production to a factory specialising in large vessels such as horticultural pottery or containers for the chemical industry. How they could be glazed and decorated was far from clear; it might not be possible at all.

I made fifteen small-scale prototypes of various forms that went together in groups of three, and contacted factories in the U.K. and in Germany. For one reason or another they all turned the idea down, but one British company gave me a verbal estimate of what a pot four feet high would have cost had they been able to co-operate, and it was far more than I had expected. Since the whole project was coming to look less and less possible it seemed only fair to telephone the architects to warn them that our meeting was likely to be a waste of time.

During the intervening weeks I had a number of telephone conversations with them, from which it emerged that they were no clearer about what they really wanted than I was about how to make it. Originally they had spoken of sixty pots; now they said it could be half that number. At one time they said the pots should be strongly coloured, but later they said they could be bone-white. They need not necessarily be glazed; the surfaces might be vapour-fumed or sand-blasted. Nor did they have to be six feet high; five feet would be enough, or even less. They wanted containers to furnish a large interior atrium, not non-functional sculptural forms, but they should have what they called a sculptural presence, and they must not be terracotta, the usual material for things of this size. There was a budget for the interior furnishings, but it was not yet certain how much could be allocated to the pots. They felt sure a solution to the technical obstacles could be worked out, but they obviously understood very little about making or firing pots of any kind. The only certain thing was that the pots must be ready in eighteen months time.

This was how matters stood when they arrived one winter evening and we went, shivering, to look at the lustre pots in the loft in the unflattering lamplight. To my surprise, the architects were extremely enthusiastic, so much so that I had to warn them before their ideas raced ahead that the third firing required for lustre would be an almost unacceptable risk for pots of the size they had in mind. To the best of my knowledge no-one had made such large lustre pots since the last Alhambra vases about six hundred years ago. I explained that anything as big as this would probably have to be unglazed, and that the making and firing might have to be sub-contracted. However, since five people from the firm had taken the trouble to come all this way, I didn't want to sound too negative; at least I could show them my small scale prototypes to prove that we had given the project some thought. Again they were enthusiastic.

"So you are interested!

"In practical possibilities, yes."

"We'd want the real thing, of course – your designs, your touch. They'd have to be made here, not sub-contracted. What would be the maximum size you could consider?"

"Probably about four feet high".

They conferred.

"It might be enough. We'd like them to be glazed, and with lustre, like the pots we saw just now. Something on the lines of the photographs you sent, which everyone admired.

"I doubt if that's possible." I reminded them of what I had explained already.

"How do you know? The pot over there must be three feet high, and you got lustre on that. Surely you can do it again?"

People often ask this, but reduction-lustre is a fickle process, and it is seldom possible to do the same thing twice.

"It might be done," I replied, " but not sixty times over. Even if we could make the pots, we couldn't store them all or fire them in the time available. Anyway, they might easily crack in the lustre firing, if we ever get that far."

"We have revised the number. We now think twenty-six would be enough. That's a big difference."

"But we don't know if we can actually make them at all," I protested.

"It wouldn't be the first risk you've taken, would it? Why not give it a try? Full scale and with lustre designs, these prototypes would be superb. You know that. Just imagine it!"

"But it's almost impossible." I was beginning to feel trapped.

"That's what we want. Something almost impossible."

Eventually I agreed that we would try to produce six pots during the summer, provided they shared the financial risk, calculating the value on the basis of the verbal estimate I had been given for unglazed pots by the factory. The costing was haphazard but there was nothing better to go on. If this pilot project worked, we would go ahead; if not, they would have to look elsewhere.

Pots of this size are unusual but some are still made today. A few artist potters hand-build them in their studios, and usually construct them on trucks which are wheeled

BIG POTS

into the kiln so that the completed piece does not have to be lifted while it is still fragile. Traditional vessels for storage and horticulture are still produced at Colmenar in Spain, at Pruneta and Ripabianca in Italy and probably elsewhere in the Mediterranean countries, and in India. But they are almost always unglazed, which means that the makers can use coarse materials that steady the clay and lessen the risk of cracking, and, of course, they require only one firing. To fire them three times, as we would have to do, entailed a great deal more work as well as the risk of losing a completed pot at the very last stage. Still, no venture, no gain. Everyone in the Pottery was keen to go for it.

The pots were made in the way I had constructed the twenty-five gallon teapot a few years before, in sections, using two wheels. On the first wheel was thrown the base, looking like a very wide bowl with shallow sides three-quarters of an inch thick. Additional sections were thrown on a wide disk on the second wheel. Each new section was lifted off on the disk, which was then turned upside down, and the two parts were then joined rim to rim. After separating off the disk with a wire the new section was re-thrown, gradually extending the height and width to the measured profile shown in the full-scale drawings based on the prototypes. And so onwards, stiffening the clay of the lower parts with a gas torch and adding and re-throwing new sections until the pot was complete. The pot could then be lifted from the wheel by three people by means of a double-bed sheet wrapped around its belly. It was then left to dry for two months before receiving its first firing, lasting two days and two nights.

To avoid the exhausting business of firing so slowly with wood in our own kiln we took the first four pots by road to a friend who kindly agreed to fire them for us in his large gas kiln, a newly-built, modern, computer-controlled structure with ceramic-fibre blanket insulation. He fired it with meticulous care and the pots cooled for three days. Through no fault of his, they all came out cracked. The damage happened not in the firing itself but as the kiln cooled. Blanket-fibre is an excellent insulation, but having little mass it does not hold its heat; the pots therefore cooled too quickly for their size and ghastly dunting-cracks developed. They were useless.

It had taken four months to get this far. Even supposing that the firing problem could be solved, there was no longer time to begin all over again and complete all the pots by the required date. I wrote to the architects to explain, apologising for having to let them down.

The news seemed to upset them a good deal, perhaps because they were genuinely keen on the idea of the big lustre pots, and perhaps partly because time was getting on and they didn't know where else to turn. At this point they said that the finished pots need not, after all, be ready by the end of the following year; so long as half of them were available by then, they could wait for the remainder. So they persuaded us to go on trying. It wasn't difficult. We had the bit between our teeth and had already figured out that by using a sandier mix of clay and acquiring a bulk-tank of gas we might manage to fire the pots to red heat very slowly in our own kiln without cracking them or losing two nights' sleep. The firing could then be completed with wood in the usual way. Our kiln was built of solid brick and therefore held its heat for several days and the pots were unlikely to crack as they cooled. So we began all over again.

The only difficulty was that at present we couldn't get the largest pots into the kiln at all. Edgar spent the next ten days enlarging the doorway. Ingeniously he severed the girders that held the sides of the kiln together and re-welded them to form a pointed archway just high enough to allow the pots to pass through. Then he and Julian converted part of the long shed into a drying room with a paved floor and metal ventilating grids on which the pots would stand as they dried. In the following winter, insulated walls and heating had to be added to protect them from frost, which can destroy undried pots in an hour.

Winter was still far away, and the late summer of that year provided perfect drying conditions for the new pots; an Indian potter had come to spend a few months with us, and we were pleased to discover that Aldermaston was sometimes slightly hotter than Bombay. Our previous disappointments had taught us some important lessons and this time the work went more smoothly. Two months later we managed to biscuit-fire three large pots with complete success. It was delightful to tap their sides as they emerged from the kiln and hear the bell-like resonance of the hard, fired clay.

The next stage was to coat them with glaze. Glazing pots of normal size is very simple; they are dusted and simply dipped in a tub in which the glaze powder is suspended in water like a thin cream. It takes just a few seconds. To glaze a pot four foot high is rather more tricky. The Alhambra vases must have had the glaze poured over them, as is shown by the places in which it has gathered, forming uneven pools and 'curtains'. It must have been extremely difficult, and we decided instead to resort to a spray-gun powered by an air-compressor. It takes a good deal of care and patience to apply the glaze with the right thickness evenly all over without bubbling, but before that the pots had to be glazed on the inside, on the places spray-guns cannot reach. To do this the pot was placed on its side on a long table and one person threw a couple of buckets of thin glaze into it while two others, on their hands and knees on the table, rolled it back and forth until the interior was completely covered. Then it had to be up-ended to pour the rest of the glaze out. It looked and felt like a circus act but it worked reasonably well in spite of the laughter and the splashing.. Then the double-bed sheet came in useful once again. I do not know how we would otherwise have lifted such large pots, covered with dry, powdery glaze, and positioned them in the kiln with an accuracy of a quarter of an inch. The second firing was less anxious work than the first. Earthenware clay contracts by about nine per cent when it is fired. The biggest pots had therefore already shrunk by nearly five inches and adjusted to the stress. Nevertheless it was a relief to see them come out safe and sound, covered in hard, shining glaze.

These pots had been thrown by the younger potters, Julian, Andrew and Sam, who had not, like me, had three hernia operations, but I had designed them and intended to paint them myself. I imagined the pots in groups of three, each pot having an individual presence and a distinct profile, colour and design.

The scale was totally unfamiliar. Sitting, or more often kneeling, close up to the pot with the loaded brush in hand, it was difficult to keep any sense of the form as a whole while attending to the detail. Before me was a vast ceramic wall beside which even my widest brush felt like a midget. The free, improvised brushwork that I had done often enough on other lustre vessels was beside the point for things of this size. Any free brushwork would have to be married to the overall form by some kind of design-structure, otherwise it would become incoherent, yet I didn't want the structure to become too formal. As Gombrich says, if a design is obvious, the mind simply doesn't register it, and if it is confused the eye resists it. I wanted designs that the mind and the eye could play with and think about. I tried to conceive them as a combination of masculine and feminine elements; as coherent structures supporting relatively mobile features without formal rules.

I spent two days on the first pot before getting anywhere, sketching possible themes with dye and again and again wiping the glaze clean with a sponge and starting afresh. Not exactly afresh, however, for by the end of that first day I was exhausted. Perhaps it was a necessary stage to go through, for when I began again the next morning the general features of the design more or less painted themselves. All I had to do was decide where to stop and what to leave out. That also takes time, but much less. By the afternoon I was painting with the lustre pigment itself and the work soon began to take hold of me. For the next three days I was absorbed in it, painting at

Top: Lifting a newly made pot with the sheet: Julian Bellmont and Andrew Hazelden, 1991.

Bottom: In the Pearl Centre, Peterborough: ACS and Andrew Hazelden, 1992.

BIG POTS

strange bodily inclinations so that the brush would spread the pigment nicely, sometimes perched precariously on a chair, sometimes kneeling on the ground, or, as it felt, standing almost on my head. By the end of the week it was done. All that was needed now was another pot of similar size to stand on the opposite side of the kiln, balancing the pull of the flames.

The first pot had taken almost a week because of all my doubts and second thoughts. The next one had a completely different kind of design and it began to come right from the very first cast. The painting progressed almost without hesitation and was completed on the second day. Both pots were soon positioned in the kiln together with things of more normal size and the firing began in the dark at 4 o' clock on a frosty morning. Since these were far and away the largest lustre pots we had ever attempted we fired slowly, taking fourteen hours instead of the usual seven, hoping that they would not crack, but still not knowing whether in the slightly uneven heat the lustre would develop properly all over them, if indeed it worked at all. The previous year there had been one firing in which hardly a single piece came out well.

Our luck held better than I had dared to hope. Pots always come out of the lustre kiln looking anything but lustrous. All you see at first is the scorched and blackened ochre in the pigment lying on the painted areas. This ochre has to be rubbed away with a cloth and if the firing is good the lustre is revealed underneath it, bonded into the glaze. On this occasion I delicately rubbed a small area on the shoulder of the first of the big pots. What was I going to find? The patch looked reddish. I rubbed again; it was very red. I rubbed more, widening the area; it was not just red, it was an iridescent, sheeny red, rich and deep and glorious. I extended the rubbing and other people came to help, working from the rim down the whole body to the foot, rubbing, wiping the dust away, and polishing. The colour was lighter lower down, but it was all good, good the whole way. Later, almost unbelievably, the second pot came out equally well.

By mid-day the two pots stood before us, clean and grand. Everything had worked. Here before us was the proof that it really could be done. It wasn't a wild goose-chase or a will o' the wisp or a pipe-dream or a shot in the dark. Here they were, touchable, ringable, standing beside us. What a day that was. What a wonderful beginning. A lot had happened since the night we shivered in the loft in the lamplight. All that remained now was to do it a dozen times more.

———

POTTERY, PEOPLE AND TIME

Sixteen months later, in April 1992, we installed the twenty-six pots in the Nene Hall Atrium at Lynch Wood. Since we couldn't store more than six of them at a time, they had been collected at intervals by a fine art removals firm, and this was the first time we had seen them all together. In that vast space they seemed at first quite small, but they held their own. Only when standing beside them did one realise that the biggest pots were considerably larger in volume than the human body. The light from the great glass vault shone down, bringing out the iridescence of the lustre, as the architects must have foreseen, but far more effectively than I had dreamed of.

Not the least of the rewards of this extraordinary commission was the reaction of the staff working in the building. Groups of people were wandering amongst the pots murmuring softly and stroking them.

19

SUNDIAL

Eventually the sundial fired beautifully. The glaze was a fat, even, warm white and the detailed painting came out clear and assured. One would never guess the troubles that lay behind the scenes. We worked on it off and on for four years.

John, a friend of ours who lives in the village, commissioned it as a retirement present to himself from his fellow directors at the Ram Brewery in Wandsworth, which was the reason for the golden ram in the centre.

The first hitch was getting the correct angles for telling the time. Anne-Marie had just done a course in navigation but it seemed ages before she managed to calculate the proper angles for the latitude of Aldermaston. I couldn't see what was against simply marking out the shadows from the fin on Midsummer's Day, but apparently this would have been incorrect. Then we made a disk nineteen inches wide from a mixture of red clay and crucible clay. What with cracking while drying, freezing in winter, explosions in the kiln, and other troubles, we had to make quite a number of disks altogether. John was very patient, and when he eventually saw the finished sundial, glazed and painted and fitted with its brass fin, he was delighted.

The sundial was steeped in silicone to prevent the absorbtion of water so that it could survive the winter frosts. It was bonded to a heavy concrete disk on top of a stone-coloured chimney-pot as a pedestal. This stood on a circular brickwork base on the lawn near the front door of John's house.

It was a warm winter. All was well until heavy frost descended in April. Evidently silicone solution loses its potency when it is stored, for moisture had penetrated the fired clay and when it froze it expanded, shaling off the glaze on the surface. The sundial looked pathetic. John was distressed. I was ashamed. Exactly the same thing happened on a larger scale to the so-called Palais de Porcelaine ordered by Louis XIV for his mistress Madame de Montespan, not that this was much consolation.

Another disk was made, this time in stoneware clay, which becomes vitreous when it is fired and therefore absorbs virtually no water. Unfortunately the clay was fine-textured and the disk split as it dried. The next one blew up in the kiln. The final one was made of a coarse, tough stoneware clay intended for large paving tiles. A friend fired it for us in his new high-tech kiln together with some very large jars, in an extra slow fifty-hour biscuit firing to 1000°C. We then fired it again to 1280°C. to make it impervious and as hard as possible. Once it had been painted and fired the brass fin was glued into place and the sundial was impregnated for three days with brand-new silicone solution.

By then it was December. John had accepted the delays philosophically and I wanted to show him the completed work as soon as possible. It was much better than the first. To make some ceremony out of the absurdity of bringing a sundial in mid-winter, I took it to him on St. Lucy's day, traditionally the shortest day of the year, and together we read Donne's *Nocturnall*.

> Tis the yeares midnight, and it is the dayes,
>   Lucies, who scarce seven houres herself unmaskes,
>   The Sun is spent.........

Special commissions often present new problems and involve more work than anyone foresees, but when they end well they are specially satisfying. I was particularly pleased with the sundial, not only because we eventually got it right, but because of its meaning.

John served in the navy during the war. Hence the Naval Crown. His corvette, Hyacinth, is commemorated by the flowers at the base of the design. The other flowers are the names of other corvettes in the flotilla. Each had a complement of about eighty men. Four of the ships survived, but H.M.S. Snapdragon, Erica and Salvia were lost in action off the coast of Libya.

John says he does not dwell on these things; they belong to the past; but the ships and the men he knew are part of his life and he could never forget them. The inscription HORAS NON NUMERO NISI SERENAS ('I count only the beautiful hours') is of course entirely right for a sundial but it has another and more poignant meaning because of those ships and all the men whose lives were lost.

It isn't just a matter of the past. Our lives would have been very different if others had not made these sacrifices for us. I was fifteen when the war ended, and I

remembered people in the armed forces saying "When all this is over I'll do something I really care about, something worthwhile. That'll be the time…" Some of them did not live to see it. Others forgot their resolve. Others could find no way of following it up, but some did. My generation grew up inheriting their outlook. Peace is not just the absence of war. It's for something.

Of course things don't necessarily work out. People can be as disappointed doing their own thing as by anything else, but many of my generation had at least to give it a try.

20

CERAMICS

One more firing to come before the next exhibition: with any luck this will add a few more special pieces to what we already have, and it could be really good. The invitation cards arrived yesterday; they are nicely done and there is an eye-catching colour-photo on the front. Nonetheless, I was sorry to see that the Gallery have titled the exhibition 'New Ceramics'. Half the exhibitions in this country are called that, and it suggests something quite different from what I have to offer.

Working with clay gives people a strong fellow-feeling. It transcends the barriers of nation and background and for me it has been a passport to unforgettable and heart-warming contacts with potters in distant places, in Morocco, in Egypt and in the jungle in Sri Lanka. In Britain potters express it by backing each other up with moral support and technical help, over and above quite deep differences of outlook.

Two radically different directions have become more and more apparent over the last three decades, here and everywhere. There are those who make pottery mainly for use, working in a variety of different styles and materials. Then there are others, now the majority in the more affluent countries, who concentrate on various kinds of non-functional work, from small conceptual forms to abstract sculptures. For them it is the material, the concept and the expression that count. Of course it is really all ceramics, since the word embraces everything made of clay, but nowadays non-functional forms are usually referred to as Ceramics and clay vessels as Pottery.

So why has the gallery called my exhibition 'New Ceramics'? Because in P.R. terms, 'Ceramics' is a word of higher status than 'Pottery'. 'Pottery' suggests repetition, and therefore a loss of uniqueness. If it can be used, the implication is that the artistic concept is not entirely dominant, whereas the label 'Ceramics' suggests unique art-objects .

Janice Tchalenko says she was once telephoned unexpectedly by the owner of a

Upper left: Antonia Salmon (U.K.).
Lower left: Kristine Michael (India).
Upper right: Jan de Rooden (Netherlands).
Lower right: Ruth Duckworth (U.K. and U.S.A.).

modern gallery in New York. He wanted some of her work for his next ceramics exhibition. "The best you have," he said, "but strictly art pieces. No lids and no handles. That makes it craft".

People have been making all kinds of things in clay from time immemorial, but 'Ceramics' in the contemporary sense began to take off in the West in the early 'sixties, with the conviction that it had a proper place in the world of contemporary fine art, which was itself in a self-consciously innovative phase. Drawing from life was being virtually eliminated and abstract expressionism seemed to show the way forward. It seemed just as relevant in ceramics as in painting.

It happened not only with ceramics but with all the other materials too, metals, wood, paper, glass, tapestry, textiles, etc. Everything was reconsidered as fabric for self-sufficient art-objects. The practical or ceremonial uses that once gave objects a place in the pattern of human life were now seen by many people as limitations, restricting free expression and inhibiting the play of the material. In this view, pottery was inevitably being superseded by ceramics, and some people saw it as a natural and inevitable historical process. A Dutch acquaintance of ours summed it up with painful directness at one of my exhibitions, explaining why he was not buying anything: "for pottery we go to the factory; for ceramics we regard the artist."

It was a bit sweeping, but I could see his point. Many people can't, like the Provençal potter Marcel, one of the best traditional craftsmen in Biot, where they have been making pots since before the Roman Empire. When I met him he had just finished an almost life-size clay model of an armchair and was wondering how to fire it. He explained that these days one has to take the bull by the horns. "These arty types can't tell one pot from another. Working on the wheel won't get you anywhere these days, but this sculpture of mine could be exhibited in Paris." He was being naive and defiant, but behind his bravado was the traditional potter's confused response to the new scenario.

Whatever Marcel may have felt, the new movement had come to stay and fascinating things have followed from it. Forms, textures and glazes not relevant to functional pottery are explored with uninhibited verve, technical inventiveness and a richness of conceptual imagination undreamed of by the traditional artisan. Non-functional ceramics have been made since the dawn of history as adjuncts to the making of vessels, but in the last hundred years, and in the last few decades especially, they have become a mainstream of boundless variety all over the world from California to Karnataka.

The physical responses and mental concepts embodied in these ceramics are not totally different from those of makers of vessels, but they take a very different direction. They lead to new and self-sufficient objects, while vessels relate to patterns of life that are already in existence. Most people who work with clay could go in either direction, but in practice it is difficult to follow two stars at the same time. "Open yourself. Re-think everything you took for granted; it only holds you back," one of our friends used to say to his pupils. An exciting course, but it doesn't suit everyone. It can generate refreshing, experimental work in quest of goals that are undefinable until they are reached, but it leaves some people at a loss. It was in fact simply a first step towards a complex reconsideration of what ceramics is about.

Alison Britton's careful notes for an exhibition catalogue indicate the depth of thought that lies behind new work in ceramics, thought that is inseparable from new methods of manipulating materials. The group she refers to here is a very wide one, not limited to any specific style, and since it includes a considerable number of people in various countries, it is worth quoting at some length.

> My work may in the future be seen to have belonged to a 'group' ...concerned with the outer limits of function; where function, or an idea of possible function, is crucial, but is just one ingredient in the final presence of the object, and is not its only motivation... Some people will certainly feel that it represents the last decadent throes of an artistic crafts movement of dwindling relevance, where over-selfconscious makers turned in on themselves for want of a real sense of necessity. But perhaps to others it will be seen as something closely in line with 'modernism' in the other arts, in painting or literature for example. A 'modern' novel (one following such writers as Proust and Joyce) is both made of, and about, language. Some of the objects I have chosen [for the exhibition] are similarly self-referential, that is, they perform a function, and at the same time are drawing attention to what their own rules are about... I would like to make a comparison evident between 'prose' objects and 'poetic' objects; those that are mainly active and those that are mainly contemplative. To me the most moving things are the ones where I experience in looking at them a frisson from both these aspects at once, from both prose and poetry, purpose and commentary. These have what I call a 'double presence'.[5]

CERAMICS

Yet self-referential ceramic art objects have their limitations. They keep their distance. Like natural formations in rocks, crystals and fungi, they remain 'other'. That is sometimes an important part of their appeal. They are mostly eye-objects rather than touch-objects, for contemplation, not for use. You can't actually do anything with them. They are a contemporary equivalent of 'objects of virtue', to be perused, not used, and kept safe. And many of them are indeed objects of virtue, in the original sense of the word, meaning power or potency.

Nonetheless, abstract expressionism and conceptualist post-modernism in ceramics can sound more progressive than they actually are. Amongst the genuinely exploratory, conceptual works are many hit-or-miss objects, sometimes diverting, but often merely idiosyncratic or ephemeral. A way-out point of departure or an ingenious handling of material does not take the place of a living and lasting idea. Unless the work stems from some sustained vision or enquiry in the maker's mind it cannot mean much to anyone else. Art colleges have tended to concentrate on aesthetic effects and the manipulation of material, all too often without considering what they convey or what they signify in their eventual locations. That question asks for a more generous approach to 'education', a deeper understanding of the imaginative impulses that underlie design and the urge to make. Creative impulses are not exclusive to designers and makers; they are shared by a great many people, though unrecognised until the emotions lying dormant in the back of the mind are awakened by the work of an artist. No communication can take place unless there is something genuine to communicate. Without it, what emerges is inevitably little more than diversion or satire.

Those who achieve outstanding works in non-functional ceramics do so through rigorous restraint, following a disciplined system of rhythm, colour, texture and proportion, always with a sustained and enquiring theme behind it, very different from some of the self-styled 'exploratory' work that regularly appears in international exhibitions. In the work of people such as Coper, Duckworth, Fritsch, de Rooden and Kvetensky nothing is random or arbitrary. It is as self-sufficient as music, and it reflects in new and unexpected ways the sense of order that is built into the human mind.

Pottery for use, on the other hand, has to accept limitations and fulfil certain needs, some of which have hardly changed for centuries. Therefore it is often disregarded by periodicals giving space to what is new. Here too, inevitably, trivial work is found alongside the pots that keep their magic, but for the best of it there is still much to be said. The range it covers is immense and potters working by hand are usually far more versatile than a factory. Their work has a place in almost every human activity from eating and drinking to ceremonies, ritual and horticulture. Its usefulness is not only a restriction, it is one of its principal assets. Because you do something with it you know it by touch, volume and balance, and you sense many things the eye can't see. The interest of non-functional ceramics is almost exclusively visual, whereas pots that are used can be appreciated even by the blind because they are perceived by the hand, the skin, the lip, not only by the eye. The pots have a place in the pattern of life. They add enjoyment and a certain ritual meaning to everyday occasions, not only to special events such as the Japanese tea-ceremony. If they are good, they have much more to them than usefulness: they are evocative companions in a world of time and change. The material is what it is, but it is no longer something other.

The Craft-Art debate is here to stay and it reflects genuinely different attitudes of mind among the makers, but it would be a pity to make too much of the difference between Ceramics and Pottery, the usable vessel and the conceptual art object, despite the militant rivalries that arise from time to time between champions of one or the other. There will always be a good deal of positive give-and-take between them. Most vessels are to some extent sculptural, and functional pottery is continually enriched by ideas and experimentation from non-functional ceramics. Whatever our line of work, we are all people of the clay, able, as the Bible puts it, 'of the same lump to make one vessel unto honour, and another unto dishonour.'

As for the loyalty between everyone who works with clay, I remember the day Michael Sellers brought Hans Coper over to the Pottery during the last year of his life, a genius in a very different field from ours. He was by then so crippled that he could scarcely get out of the car, but he suddenly asked to be helped up and stood unsteadily beside us, looking around him. 'Now at last,' he remarked, 'I can say that I have set my feet on the ground at Aldermaston'. The gesture of solidarity stays in my mind. He was affirming a bond that exists between all clay-people, over and above their differences of outlook. Basically, and at our best, we are all concerned with metaphors of life.

21

SKILL

The other day Anne-Marie came home with a bundle of table-mats. We had plenty of such things already, but she said these were irresistible. The bundle consisted of eight mats made of fine, hand-cut slivers of bamboo and a tough, smooth reddish-black reed, woven into an ingenious design of crosses and diamonds. They were thin, tough and pliable, a pleasure to touch. Every sliver was perfect. Attached to them was a paper neatly inscribed in Thai writing. When Anne-Marie happened on them in the Oxfam shop she was immediately won over. The bundle cost £3.60. "It makes you think," said the woman in the shop. "How do they live?"

We have thought a good deal since then, not only about the price, but about the skill and patience that went into the work. A printed message explained that the village craftsmen have for ages past woven the same materials to cover the sides and floors of their timber-framed houses. These mats were the same kind of weave done on a small scale to earn Western currency. They were not simply attractive ethnic artefacts. There was more to them and they fascinated us. Everything that is perfectly made has something to say over and above what it is in itself. The mats were modest, but they had an integrity that conveyed something of a dignified natural order, the kind of order you see in a snowflake or the tissue of a leaf, or a feather. The fabric was beautiful too, but it was also something of a shock.

A shock because today this kind of craftsmanship, depending on skills perfected by generations of practice, can hardly any longer be matched in the west. For better or worse, our pattern of life and our way of thinking have taken a different direction. The woven bamboo is one of the innumerable traditional skills that have developed across the globe from time immemorial, usually because the products are needed, but sometimes simply as a way of passing time or keeping out of mischief. I have in the house another example, a most extraordinary one. It's a Japanese painting-brush from the Otokoyama Mountain, made by meticulously dividing the fibres of a piece of bamboo until, unbelievably, they become as soft and flexible as hair. The maker's note says it is done 'by hand work of very experienced craftsman carefully, taking a long time'. Who in the western world has the patience to learn such a skill? Yet it still happens in Japan. The note continues:

> Since 1,000 years ago Japanese use this brush, for calligraphy and Japanese paint and this brush create the beautiful lines and crespy feeling but yet very soft with you. I beleave you will enjoy and falling love with this Bamboo brush, once you experienced.

I've seen another example of this kind of skill in a potter's kiln near Cairo, filled with unglazed water-pots, hundreds and hundreds of them, placed on their sides one above another, alternately base forward and top forward. They fit most beautifully together. I've seen Sambo, the potter, making them. It's done in two stages: the upper half is made first, leaving the base very thick; after the pot has dried a little it is put back on the wheel the other way up and the thick clay is re-thrown to form the lower half of the pot and then closed in to form the bottom. Sambo has been making five hundred of these pots every week since he was fourteen. He is now nearly forty, so he must have made at least three quarters of a million.

These craftsmen were never trained in the western sense of the term. Few of them ever attended a school. They grew up in the family workshop, and as Said El Sadr said, 'Here at least they learn something'. They worked alongside their elders day after day until the best of them became amazingly expert. The Oxfam lady's question 'how do they live?' is very much to the point. It's not surprising that most of them are poor. If their life-style had not been simple and monotonous, they would never have reached this astonishing fluency. It comes from a clear-cut, unquestioning background: 'This is how it is done'. No doubts, no revisions, no alternatives. This kind of craftsman and the craftsman designers of the west are almost incomprehensible to each other.

Yet paradoxically, the greater the gulf between the modern west and the environment of traditional craftsmen, the greater the inspirational value of the things they make.

A few years ago an American lady, Mrs Vanderbilt Webb, had an inspiration while walking in the cool of the evening on the coast of Sri Lanka. She described how that afternoon she had watched the manufacture of batiks and repoussé silverware in some local workshops and had been astonished that the craftsmen knew nothing of anything

SKILL

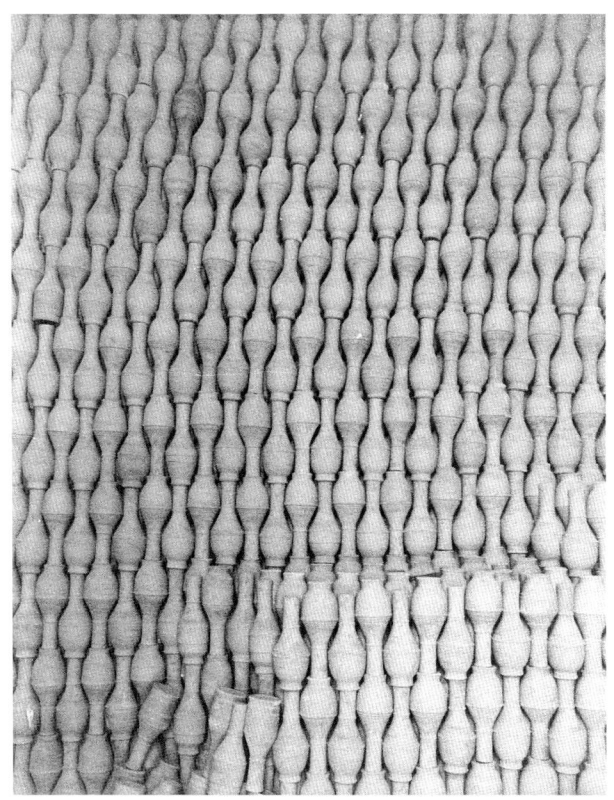

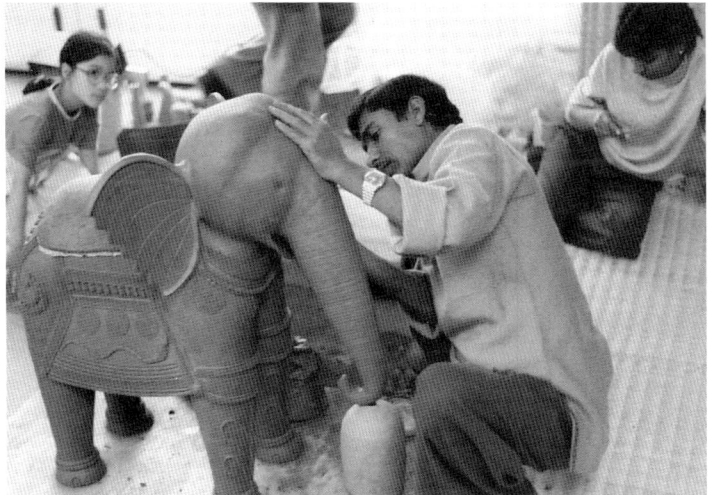

Top: Water bottles, stacked in a kiln, Fustat, Egypt, 1980.
Bottom: In the Indian Festival, London, 1982.

being done in other parts of the world. Nor did they know anything of the materials and equipment that would be taken for granted in the most elementary classes in the U.S.A. Suddenly she felt she had a mission: she would establish a World Crafts Council, through which the craftsmen of the world would be put in touch with one another; they would exchange technical information and share experience and imagination. It was a bold idea and the movement received a good deal of support. It seemed obvious that all these people could not fail to benefit one another. The organisation was founded with a splash of international publicity and continues to this day, though I have always felt that the idealism was top-heavy. In the early days, there was a large open meeting at the Victoria and Albert Museum, where many enthusiastic statements were exchanged. Towards the end of the proceedings, however, a man from Ethiopia made the most memorable contribution. He said simply "My people cannot read or write. They would not understand you. If you wish them well, you will leave them alone."

There was an embarrassed silence. Leave the people poor and backward? This was not the idea at all. They were meant to learn to help themselves to advance. But he spoke from experience. Not only in Ethiopia but throughout the world, traditional skills are strong but they are also very vulnerable. If the methods or the designs are changed, the makers lose their bearings, because these things were not chosen, as a Western designer-craftsman chooses. They were 'given' and learned without comparison or analysis. The re-thinking that looms so large in western craft and design simply doesn't enter. This kind of work didn't start from planned designs; it evolved over centuries on the basis of 'this is how it is done'. Tradition governs not only techniques and materials, but the forms and designs as well. Many of them are derived from tribal customs and have age-old ceremonial uses; others incorporate ritual emblems and prophylactic signs passed down over the generations. Symbols of this sort are inherited and they have to be remembered correctly because they are the links with the intangible world. 'This is the way it has to be'. The Ethiopian understood what was at stake. To dilute this kind of tradition means destroying it.

This is difficult for us to understand, for in the West the maker usually designs and chooses what he produces and it bears the stamp of his individuality. But the traditional craftsman is first and foremost a provider of familiar things for use or ornament; he accepts current uses and conventions, and his work is endlessly repetitive. Personal imagination doesn't come into it.

At the Indian Festival in London a few years ago a young potter demonstrated the clay animal figures he made for festivals in his village. When we arrived he was making an elephant about two feet high, fashioning the parts and assembling them slowly and certainly into an elaborate and perfectly finished figure. It had little money value. We were told, in fact, that the figures were usually never fired but put in the river after the festival and turned back to mud. All the same, as with many ethnic artefacts, there was a big idea behind it. The animal figures were for the god to ride on, bringing blessings to the people. A journalist asked the potter if he ever made anything different. 'Sometimes', he replied, ' when the goddess comes in a dream and shows me something new. Then I can'.

People often assume that repetition is drudgery, thinking of the excesses of the industrial revolution, the 'Song of the Shirt', and the sweat shops of present-day Manila, Bangkok, and New York and the persistent, ghastly exploitation of underpaid labour. But not all repetitive work is drudgery. There are kinds of repetitive craftsmanship that bring dignity and ease of mind and sometimes inspiration.

For instance, I remember seeing a film a few years ago about an Algerian comb-maker. He worked in the street making combs from bones, slowly cutting the teeth of the comb with a little bow-saw on a portable frame. Someone suggested that it must be desperately monotonous. 'It may seem so from outside," he said, "but if the work is done as it should be done then every part of it has something to teach. From many years and many combs you come to understand things better. About God and the world, and your place. People say it's a hard way to make a living, but that's nonsense. No-one can 'make' a living. It has already been made for us. It's here now. It costs very little, even less than a comb.' He was an unusual man. Was he only a comb maker? We seemed to be on the frontier of a mystery. His words reminded me how different the narrow field of a specialised skill may be from what it seems.

Brilliant specialist craftsmen don't belong only to the Third World. The most extraordinary pottery thrower of this century was probably Harold Thomas, who worked for Buller's Ltd. in Stoke-on-Trent. The Company's advertisements used to include pictures of him at work, making giant electrical insulators and enormous porcelain jars considerably taller than himself. Towards the end of his career he was lent to a London theatre company, who wanted to have a potter working back-stage to add colour to a production of *Ali Baba and the Forty Thieves*. Harold asked what he should make. 'Anything you like', said the producer, 'but big enough to be seen by the people at the back'. Despite his shyness and the turban and galabeia in which they dressed him up he did so well that he became the main attraction. After the first two performances the producer had to ask him to make something less exciting: the audience was complaining that the actors kept getting in the way.

These highly skilled artisans are often unacknowledged in the West today because of the emphasis placed on creativity and self-expression. They don't appear to be creative in the sense given to the word in a modern schoolroom. Therefore it's often considered that they have little to do with real, creative work.

You can see why. Since we have devised brilliant machinery to perform repetitive work better and quicker than we could possibly do it ourselves, why waste energy on it? It is assumed, wrongly I believe, that the repetitive work of a skilled artisan is equally automatic and devoid of thought. This assumption carries weight partly because today many people become involved in a craft not as a professional training but as a leisure activity or as a branch of liberal education. They don't want to spend a long time acquiring a skill before getting results. Learning a skill is a slog, but having ideas is fun and relatively quick. It is easy to feel that taking trouble is not virtuous but just silly. Easy to feel too that making things that work or solving technical problems is a chore that artists shouldn't have to bother about because the proper line for the creative person is the original, self-expressive, non-functional art object. It can't be put to a practical test and it may fetch a good price.

There's an element of sense in this way of thinking. Too much hard, repetitive work can all too easily blockade new ideas. The hard labour imposed by the traditional crafts of the Third World would drive the innovative designer-maker crazy, but the fact remains that skilled understanding of material is a basic necessity in giving form to an idea. Most of the creative geniuses of our civilization were also accomplished technicians, Leonardo da Vinci being the outstanding example, but there have been plenty of others nearer our own time, Wren and Brunel, Walter Gropius and Paul Klee, indeed Picasso himself, who when he chose could manipulate clay like a magician.

Can any skill ever be acquired without repetition? It seems unlikely. Lions have to learn to hunt and kingfishers have to practice fishing again and again; they have just so much time and energy to get it right. If they don't, they die. So it's hardly surprising that dancers, writers, musicians, painters and others also have to learn their craft or art the hard way. A potter has to attempt the same shape again and again, compare the forms, see the differences and learn the appropriate lifts and rhythms. Control depends upon skill and skill upon repetition and it cannot be dodged, though it is not necessary to equal Sambo's high total. In fact it may be important not to. Fluent repetition brings the traditional artisan reward and respect, but for those who want to develop new things as well as repeating older ones it can be a snare. After all, however ancient the forms of the woven mats, the brushes and the waterpots may be, they didn't descend out of thin air. Somebody imagined them long ago.

Designer-makers are an ancient breed, already long established in the days of the Roman Empire and continuing through changing circumstances into the present day. They have always found ways of extending their repertoire and redeveloping skills that are in danger of becoming habitual. For instance, imitating or re-interpreting designs which already existed in other media, experimenting with new materials, or taking risks where the traditional craftsman would play safe, and above all by introducing direct experience from life into their work. Makers who didn't do anything of this kind stayed where they were, and have always done so, thinking in terms of individual objects, a water-pot, a tile or an emblem, seeing only what it is, not what it might be.

To help myself to understand the difference between these two attitudes of mind, I can take the musical analogy of sonata form. The structure consists of three movements, first a melodic theme, a variation of the theme, and a contrasting passage; then a development of these three together, and finally a recapitulation, after which there is a return to the original starting point. Thus the whole sonata with all its variations and transitions is still a unified whole. It is a piece of musical architecture. The comparison indicates what the designer-maker is about, while the traditional artisan simply repeats the first melody.

To take a particular example, the wonderful Iznik tiles in the Mosque of Rüstem Pasha in Istanbul could be seen as a ceramic equivalent of sonata-form. There you see the perfect workmanship of each separate tile, but also a multitude of contrasting forms, rhythms and colours, all playing their part in a brilliant composition and making a unique spirit of place. This unforgettable building displays the different roles of the tile-painters on the one hand and the designer-maker on the other. Combined, their skills amount to a supreme, monumental work of art. The painters could never have conceived of it, while the designer could not himself have made a single tile as perfectly as a specialist painter.

Yet this is not quite the end of this line of thought. Traditional skills may be very limited in their range, but they can still be deep. Sometimes a single object, such as a tile or a jar or a few lines on a piece of paper or a woven fabric, or a mat of woven reed is so complete, so utterly right, that it goes beyond design. The maker is the instrument through which it came into existence, but not the source. When skill is totally fulfilled, the scale doesn't matter. One is looking into the centre of things, where, mysteriously, the part and the whole can't be separated. (In the concept of fractals, the entire structure is implicit even in the smallest particle). Blake perceived the mystery long ago, seeing 'a world in a grain of sand', and 'eternity in an hour'. Possibly the comb-maker and numbers of other skilled artisans have perceived it too.

This is why I bow to the weavers of those small mats, though they will never be aware of it and might not understand even if they knew.

22

CLAY

The quantity of clay in the earth's surface is almost inconceivable. In the Mississippi delta alone the clay is six miles deep and about two million tons more is deposited every day. Very few of the earth's clays, however, are the slightest use for pottery. In the less developed parts of the world potters still devote as much as a quarter of their time to locating and preparing suitable clay.

Every kind of ceramic manufacture requires clay of a particular kind. Pot-clays and brick-clays are very different and clay for throwing is different again from clay for handbuilding or casting. The clay from which an ordinary modern plate is made could not be worked on the potter's wheel and the material of an ancient storage jar or a modern flower pot could not be used for glazed ware. A Persian lustre flask would have liquified in a Chinese porcelain kiln.

Few contemporary potters in the Western world have ever dug clay from the ground. They obtain it from supply companies who prepare and modify the raw material and provide data about its properties. In most of the developed countries a wide range of prepared clay bodies is available and potters can take their pick. But since the suppliers have to concentrate on whatever is most in demand, the majority of prepared clays are for stoneware, porcelain and white industrial earthenware. Anyone wishing, like us, to work with relatively fusible earthenware clays for tin-glaze maiolica finds that the suppliers' offerings are far from ideal.

Initially we used red Staffordshire marl clays because they were easily available, even though they were dark and had to be fired at a temperature at which some of the painted colours became weak. We did better with a more fusible natural red clay from Fremington in Devonshire, a material well known to West Country slipware potters in the last century. Curiously, its chemical analysis shows that it could not have evolved from any rocks in the British Isles. The parent rocks are in Newfoundland and Nova Scotia and the clay was deposited by glaciers when Europe and North America still formed a single land-mass. It was good for our purposes except that it fired too dark for the white glazes and it matured within an inconveniently small range of temperature. If it was even slightly too hot it warped or bloated. We saw that ideally we ought to prepare our own material, as most potters did in the past.

For centuries, painted tin-glaze wares have been made from pale buff, yellowish or pink clays rich in calcium. Piccolpasso called them *genga* and his drawings in the *Three Books of the Potter's Art* show people on the banks of the river Metauro gathering the clay brought down by the winter floods. An attractive quality of these clays is that the calcium in them helps the glaze to melt and leads to a dense, pearly whiteness. We felt that if this could be achieved in Piccolpasso's day, it should be possible to do it again, at least as well, four centuries later.

It seemed simple enough: one had only to find a suitable calcareous clay, blend it with red clay and discover the best proportion. This is still done in a good many continental pottery factories, such as Makkum in Friesland, where the Tichelaar family have for three hundred years been blending local red clay and lime marl from Valenciennes. The English delftware potteries of the eighteenth century did something similar with clays from Kent and East Anglia. Their material was rather brittle, but it was reasonable to suppose that with modern knowledge and equipment one could achieve something better.

It was an attractive practical, commercial proposition. It also entailed prospecting for clay and getting close to the sources of a substance which, to me, has always seemed beautiful and extraordinary.

The first stage was to find the most suitable English deposits of calcareous clay. There are two principal geological types. First, the clays formed by the Chalk Sea of the Cretaceous period, lying in a horseshoe-shaped arc extending north, south and west of the Thames, a vast deposit which reappears across the Channel and underlies much of the battlefront of the 1914-1918 war. Secondly, the Boulder Clays in the north-east of the country, deposited by the melting glaciers that once extended into what is now the North Sea.

We obtained samples of several Yorkshire Boulder Clays currently being dug for brick making. They were pleasing to work with but unfortunately they all fired medium red: the original deposits must have been impregnated with iron-rich clays and would have had to be considerably modified to achieve the qualities we wanted.

CLAY

From the Chalk Sea arc I collected calcareous clay from an impressive, steep-sided pit near Aylsford in Kent. After screening it became fine, soft and plastic and fired to a pale yellow-buff colour. The pots made from it took the tin glaze beautifully and fired hard, without any crazing, at an acceptable temperature of 1060°C. Fired higher, the glaze developed an intriguing pink speckle which I had seen in eighteenth century English delftware; it probably occurs because of trace elements of chrome in seashells in the ancient marine sediments. Aylsford gault, as it is called, was one of the ingredients of the body used by the potteries of Southwark and Rotherhithe in the seventeenth and eighteenth centuries. Blended with our local red clay, it seemed likely to produce just the qualities we wanted. Unfortunately the owners of this magnificent pit soon afterwards sold it for infilling with rubbish, a more lucrative business than selling the clay.

Gault clays are found in many places on the Chalk Sea arc and we obtained a number of additional samples. Unfortunately, most of these turned out completely differently from the Aylsford material. Several of them even fired dark red. I had failed to understand that gault is a general name for seams of clay in this geological system and that the calcareous clays occur only in the upper layers. Armed belatedly with this knowledge, I began to investigate the upper deposits, laid down by the rising and falling of the ancient sea. The strata can be clearly seen in the cliffs at Folkestone, where the Channel slices across them.

The difficulty was to find places where the clays are exposed. They used to be dug for the manufacture of yellow bricks, still extensively seen in Kent and East Anglia, but these have now been almost entirely superseded by red bricks from the massive deposit known as the Oxford clays, lying several hundreds of feet thick between Oxford and Peterborough. Only a few of the old yellow-clay pits are still accessible. We obtained samples from several of these places. Some were too coarse and chalky to be any use, but the clays from Otford, Kent and Arlesey, Bedfordshire looked promising. We screened them, tested their plasticity, measured the water absorbtion, and blended them in graded proportions with our Fremington clay.

The results were disappointing. These samples did not have at all the same properties as the original Aylsford clay although they had the same geological origin. The Arlesey clay was much less fusible: it was near-white and porous and the glaze crazed on it, while the more plastic yellow-firing Otford clay was highly fusible, contracted by 15% in the firing, and warped to an alarming degree. An expert explained to me that the clay layers of this geological system contained widely differing proportions of clay minerals such as illite, kaolinite and smectite. These variations resulted in the formation during firing of differing phases of kaolinite-calcite minerals such as wollastonite, gehlenite, larnite and anorthic plagioclases. Interesting though this was, it was taking me out of my depth. Besides, even had I known more mineralogy, it still wouldn't have been much help in actually locating the material. It seemed preferable to concentrate on the empirical properties, which was, after all, the way good clays had been found in the past.

While persevering with the tests of calcareous gault clays of local origin, it seemed sensible to find out what blends of clay were being used by potters making tin-glazed wares elsewhere, in France, Spain or Italy. I chose Spain, partly from affection, partly because some of the best and strongest tin-glaze pottery that I knew had been made there. That autumn I visited a number of potteries in Andalucia.

All the potters I met were doing just what I had in mind, blending a red and a calcareous clay to make a strong material firing to various shades of buff, pink and pale red. None of them could explain why. "It has always been done," they said. At Bujalance the potter had recently retired but the people in the bar told me the red clay came from the field opposite and the white clay was in a *barranca* behind the garage. It belonged to Ramón, who was inside having a coffee. He fetched a spade and we gathered samples into my bag. Apparently the potters used to blend the clays fifty-fifty, "sometimes more," he said, "sometimes less, depending on the colour." The technology could have been more lucid, but it had charm.

At La Rambla there was some very pale clay, used in one pottery for making beautiful unglazed water-bottles fired with straw. The potters who made glazed wares blended this with red clays in a proportion of one to two and it came out pink. The blended clay was normally bisque-fired at 1050°C but the pale clay on its own needed to go to 1100°C. Most of the potteries still sieved the liquid clay by hand and let it dry out in sun-dried vats, but the most enterprising of the proprietors had invested in a second-hand Italian filter-press for refining the clay and de-watering it. Wages were continually rising, he said, and the old, labour-intensive method of preparing the clay would soon be out of the question. But for the press he would soon have to depend on prepared clay supplied in bags from Barcelona. "Lousy stuff, and devilishly expensive."

The Granados pottery in Lucena was a most pleasing place and the family had been there for eight generations or more. About nine people were working there, making painted tin-glaze vessels of excellent design, from a blend of red and white-firing clays, and green-glazed pots made of the white clay alone. They fired with wood at between

CLAY

Top: Hillside near Jaen: red clay loam on the lower slopes, white clay on the hill above.
Bottom: Drying clay, Safi, Morocco, 1986.

950-1000°C. Watching them throwing, I could see what an agreeable clay it was. Here they still sieved by hand and left the liquid clay to stiffen in settling tanks in the courtyard, but they were intending to install a filter-press, for the same reasons as the potter at La Rambla. The raw material, from which they gave me samples, came from the hillside about a mile outside the town.

At Arjonilla the helpful potter gave me part of a block of the white clay that he blended with the coarser red from the field below his house. The red clay is everywhere, he said, but the white is very special. It is found only in a quarry high up on the hill. The block of clay was even and clean, almost pure white. I crushed a little of it in the palm of my hand, spat on it and rubbed with my finger. It was sticky, plastic and very fine. My appreciation pleased him. "Everyone wants stuff like this," he commented, "but this kind is the very best." What struck me was that it looked quite different from the clay I had seen in England. It was completely even, with no sign of layering.

At Ubeda there were once a hundred potteries. Today only half a dozen remain along a wide road on the east side of the town, away from the prevailing wind. I was welcomed by the enterprising Paco Tito, who, like me, fires with wood. Here too they used a blend of red and white clays, mixed two parts to one, but he said that in the past the potters used a pure, off-white clay from a deposit that was now exhausted. It fired very hard at as little as 950°C. and was better than anything now available. He brought out a sherd of the old ware, with a perfect tin glaze, and gave me a small lump of the raw clay to add to my collection of samples. It resembled the beautiful clay I had seen at Arjonilla.

One of the best days of all was spent at Baen with José de la Torre, who forgave me for rousing him from his siesta and shared his bread and fruit. His place was something of a mess, though he was very productive. He was on his own now, he said. His son had worked with him for several years but gave it up to become a plumber. Times were uncertain. For proper pots "no hay ambiente", there was no longer any call, since people had running water and refrigerators. He was fifty-nine, too old to change, but a few people were still buying. He insisted I should try his wheel and we passed the afternoon showing each other how we worked. He gave me pots to take home and we drank wine. He too prepared his own mix of red and white clay, sieving it into sun-dried vats in the old way, and gave me samples. Did glazes go well on it? He didn't know. Had I ever tried glazes? He had done his best and eventually gave them up. He pointed to a heap of pots covered with dark, crusty dribbles. "Glazes are the devil!"

Were these whitish Spanish clays different from ours, and if so, in what way? In Granada there was a chance to find out. I was told about the doyen of a celebrated family of potters who had spent a lifetime in the business and was also said to have been a professor. He knew all there was to know, but he was a busy man. His secretary told me to write down my questions. He would study them and give me the answers tomorrow. The next day he was too busy; we made an appointment for the day following. He showed me his pots and sculptures and told me of his exhibitions. Apparently he had been *sumamente* successful. His work was in national collections. Everyone had wanted his guidance as a teacher, but his art had to come first. As I would observe, his art was continually developing; creativity based on sound technology. Materials must be fully understood, alternatives tested. Young people expect to have it all on a plate. Only practice shows the way... My questions? The white clay? The answers were all available, but it was a complex matter... Of the white clay there were many varieties. He gave me a large block to take home. This one was typical, though not the best. My interesting questions... He perused the written list. Today there was not time enough for these complex studies. We would meet at ten tomorrow and he would explain everything.

When the time came his secretary said he had other essential meetings but he would be free early next week. I had by then to be in Valencia.

At La Ceramo in Benicalap, on the outskirts of Valencia, the Ros family made fine lustreware based on historic originals, from a mixture of seven parts buff clay from the Rio Turia and one part of white clay, which was unlike anything I saw elsewhere. The white clay came from a mine in the hills and they said it was rare. When I returned to England the analysis showed that it was 48.5% calcium carbonate, an astonishingly high proportion. At Talavera and Puente del Arzobispo the clay was orange rather than red but they followed the general practice of blending it with the white. The orange clay must have differed considerably from the Andalucian clays, for it was bisque-fired unusually high, at 1100°C. Most of the potteries I visited fired the bisque between 960-1050'C. Everyone, including the Talavera potters, glazed at a lower temperature, usually around 960°C., much lower than is usual in northern Europe.

A United Nations geological research team whom I happened to meet at a bar in Tangier explained to me that the clays of Morocco are virtually a mirror image of those of Andalucia, separated by the cleavage of the Straits of Gibraltar. At Salé there were several potteries employing the expected red and white clays and nearby was a large quarry in which the clay strata were clearly visible, just as the geologists had said. At Safi much of the pottery was made from a dark red clay but Kioukiou Mohamed explained that this was only used for the cheapest, common wares. The better ones were made from blended clays. He said that the Algerian master potter El Amali, who revived decorated tin-glaze pottery in Safi at the beginning of the century, had devised a pale yellow-buff blend which was about sixty per cent calcareous clay. Mohamed gave me a prized example of El Amali's work.

At Fez they used a fine-grained clay which resembled what I had seen at Arjonilla and Ubeda but they did not screen it sufficiently. As a result the elaborately painted blue, green and yellow wares were often pocked. Particles of lime in the body, turning to quicklime during the firing, absorb moisture and expand, shaling off the glaze leaving a crater. This is one of the well known snags of calcareous clays and it occurs fairly often in older wares but I had never before seen the defect so bad. When I met Abdul Hassan I understood why. He was a gentle, middle-aged man with patient eyes and a greying spade-beard around his face, and he was allocated the unenviable job of sieving the clay. Using an old saucepan, he was scooping the slurry from an immense vat and passing it through a defective screen into a series of tubs, which were then left in the sun and wind to evaporate the water. Inevitably, bits of lime passed through the sieve and more impurities settled in the clay as it dried. Often, he said, they made him sieve it all over again, several times, day after day. The wastage was enormous and if labour had not been so cheap they would have provided decent equipment years ago. Looking around to make sure no-one was watching, Hassan suddenly went down on his knees in front of me, clasping my hands. "Take me back to England," he pleaded. "You will be my master and I will serve you well." Inevitably, I had to leave him behind.

Back in England the samples were submitted to X-ray diffraction analysis and scanning electron microscopy at the British Museum Research Laboratory. With the exception of the rare clay from Benicalap and the sample from the Professor, the calcareous clays were found to consist of between 21% and 30% calcium carbonate. The detailed analyses will help to determine the provenance of historic pottery by means of trace element fingerprinting but they were not particularly informative from my point of view. Even today it is almost impossible to predict closely from an analysis how a given material will perform in practice.

During our conversations in the laboratory, however, Michael Tite, who was then the Director, told me that one of his recent research projects had shown that red and calcareous clay used to be blended for fine pottery in Anatolia and Greece around 500 B.C. and later for Roman Samian ware, for quite definite reasons. The gist of it was that the calcareous clays stabilise red clays by limiting their firing shrinkage and preventing the formation of gaseous blisters, and in cooling they increase the contraction of the vessel so that the relatively fusible engobes on the surface do not shale off. For me, the report made fascinating reading.[6] It explained why the Spanish potters used blended clays though they themselves no longer knew the reason.

It was humbling to recognise that what we were trying to do had been familiar to potters over two thousand years ago, but it was also reassuring to learn why it made technical sense.

At this point I was reminded about Boyton by Frank Britton. Boyton is a small town on the Suffolk coast from which calcareous clay was exported to Holland around 1670. The owners of the pits were accused of supplying fuller's earth to foreign competitors in the wool trade, thus infringing English protective legislation. They proved in court that Boyton clay was exported only for pottery manufacture. Frank obtained samples for me from the original pit, which has been disused for nearly two hundred years. I prepared it and made pots from it. They fired hard and true and took the glaze well at 1040°C., just like the best clays I had seen in Spain. The material produced none of the problems I had encountered with the other English calcareous clays. The Dutchmen had obviously known their business. Unfortunately the Boyton pits were long ago turned into rubbish dumps. They are now full and the clay is no longer exposed.

I understood at last that though the calcium content of the Chalk Sea clays, the Boyton clay and the Andalucian clays was roughly the same, their geological origin must be very different; therefore their mineral structure would be different and this would explain why they fired differently. I still do not know the origin of the Boyton clay, though I think it is probably a fairly pure Boulder Clay. I soon learnt, however, that most of the Andalucian and Moroccan calcareous clays are Miocene deposits originating from the chemical decomposition of earlier Jurassic limestones. A technical research report, analysing the suitablity of various calcareous Andalucian clays for ceramic manufacture, was published by a group of Spanish scientists shortly after my visit.[7] The research they had done in Andalucia was exactly what I had originally hoped to do in England. I saw now that it needed knowledge and equipment that I did not possess, but even so it was uplifting to discover that someone else had thought such a project worth while. This article answered all the questions that had not been answered by the man in Granada. If only it had appeared a few years earlier!

Since our efforts to find suitable English calcareous clays had not borne fruit, we had already tried modifying the red clay with various non-plastic materials, talc, whiting and syenite. As a result of going to Spain I thought particularly of dolomite (the double carbonate of calcium and magnesium). Like the Andalucian clays, dolomite derives from the chemical decomposition of certain kinds of limestone. If one added dolomite to the raw clay and screened the mixture before de-watering the clay in the filter-press, would it come out something like the Andalucian blended clays? The trials went well. The added dolomite did not noticeably diminish the plasticity of the clay. It made it slightly less fusible, necessitating a slightly higher firing, and it stablised it. There was no warping or cracking or bloating after firing to 1050°C. As the proportion of dolomite was increased from 5% to 25% the colour varied from a pleasing light red to pink to a yellow buff. At the temperatures we found most convenient, the best proportion of dolomite proved to be around 10%. Biscuit fired at 1000°C. and glazed at 1040°C., this clay took the glazes perfectly and no crazing developed. It proved to be a sound and delightful material and we soon fell in love with it. Potters from France, Germany and Holland have used it here and say that they know no earthenware clay to equal it.

We could at this stage have started a whole new series of tests. It would have been interesting to try out alternative local red clays, most of which are much improved by additions of dolomite and flint. This could have been of practical importance to other potters who, like us, find that the range of earthenware clays on the market is inadequate. For the moment, however, we had done enough and everyone's patience was beginning to run out. The priority now was to make good use of the blend of clay we had been lucky enough to discover.

In the end it was all so simple. Ignorance, optimisim, romanticism and bad luck all played some part in prolonging the time it took, but there were strokes of fortune too and I learned, incidentally, a great deal about clay and clay-places at close quarters, shared the experience and enthusiasm of many other potters, and acquired an immense respect for the potters of time past who achieved sound material without any of the equipment or information we count on today. One thing is certain: we would never have learned so much nor appreciated our beautiful clay half so well if we had got it right first time.

The above is a condensed account of the various lines of enquiry that were pursued, rightly or wrongly. Of the many people who provided much needed advice and practical help I would like particularly to thank the following:

Southern Arts, for financial assistance, Frank Britton, David Castillejo, Dr. Brian Causton, Peter Dick, Adrian Halstead, Frank Hamer, Dr. Michael Hughes (British Museum Research Laboratory), Dr. George Jackson (Dept. of Geology, North Staffordshire Polytechnic), Dr. Angela Jones (Dept. of Soil Science, Reading University), Jonathan Kingdon, David Lyon (Redland plc.), Dr. Ray Milburn, Dr. Stephen Nortcliffe (Dept. of Soil Science, Reading University), Colin Pearson, Natacha Seseña (Madrid), Richard Slee, Dr. T.A. Smith (British Ceramic Research Association), Pieter Tichelaar (Kongl. Aardewerk Fabriek, Makkum), Dr. Michael Tite (British Museum Research Laboratory), Mr. M. Willy (Ibstock Brick plc, Otford), and especially Nigel Wood.

Top: Lustre bowl with vapoured pigment, ACS 1994.
Bottom: Lustre jar, amber-silver on greyed glaze, painted with a cotton thread, ACS 1974.

23

DECORATION

As a student I was made to feel that colour and decoration were not only literally superficial, in that they covered a surface, but were morally superficial too and could only appeal to a degenerate sensibility, while 'pure form' expressed the nobler sides of human nature. There may be a grain of truth in this, but it's a strange view to take considering that over the last few thousand years most of the world's pottery has been decorated and much of it is beautiful and inspiring. The impulse to decorate seems to be as universal as the desire to dance or make footprints in the sand.

Some years ago, on a railway journey in Spain, I was carrying a plain white tin-glaze flask I had bought in Granada. My travelling companions could not wait to see it and it had to be passed around everyone in the carriage. Eventually the man beside me announced "The form is good, but it's a pity the potter never completed it." Actually the form was very pleasing in itself, but I knew what he meant. It was a shame to miss the opportunity. Decoration is fun; it explores form, just as bare feet discover the sea-sand. It adds something to it, just as words add to songs and songs to words.

There are songs without words and there are pots without any decoration. 'Complete' undecorated pots are amongst the subtlest of all ceramics. Some of Hans Coper's work comes to mind, and from ages past one can think of the jars of the T'ang and Yueh dynasties, whose plain surfaces suggest all possible decoration to the mind's eye. The more you look, the more you see, though none of it is actually stated.

Decorated pottery spells it out; it comes to meet you. It too has its space and silence but they appear in other ways, in between the shapes and movement. Without those vital spaces a design becomes incoherent, like wordsrunalltogetheronapage. Not all pots want to be decorated; some forms are complete in themselves. When one raises a brush beside them they silently protest "Leave us alone!" But certain forms are made to be decorated and they invite line and rhythm, imagery or pattern or inscriptions . Amongst them are classic vessels such as the Korean mae pyong prunus vase, the Persian ewer, the Italian albarello and the English punch-bowl.

Decoration is not only shapes, texture and movement but also colour, which gives it a particular emotional mood. If the colour of a design is changed it feels quite different, just as a musical theme changes its effect when it shifts into another key. Most people respond to colour as directly as they do to weather, and colour in ceramics is highly evocative – dry desert-ochres, blues royal or smoky-soft, cool greens with mysterious glassy depths, the dark bite of iron-browns, the shifting iridescence of lustre.

Our language has played tricks with the word decoration. The word has come to suggest something inessential, an afterthought, which is grossly inadequate for the best ceramics, and amounts to an inversion of the word's original meaning, which is to 'bestow honour.' Even so, there is an intriguing and quite important difference between the meaning of 'decoration' and 'decorative'. Decorative objects are mostly intended for a particular environment, such as a room furnished in a certain style, a living room, board-room or country kitchen, while a decorated object has a presence and counts in its own right wherever it is. Things that are only decorative pass on their message quite quickly, while true decoration has more to it than meets the eye and the appreciation matures with time. The eye follows the movement of line and colour, while the mind discovers contrasts, tensions and repose. Figurative or abstract, such decoration takes on meanings. It incorporates what psychiatrists call 'positive non-verbal signals'. It awakens intuitions and leaves space for the unknown.

This difference between decoration and the decorative will probably always be imprecise and will always remain something of a mystery. It underlies the whole of Gombrich's book *The Sense of Order*[8] and one chapter is devoted to these 'frontiers between ornament and symbol'. They are less subjective than one might suppose. Each has its proper place in ceramics, and most people who decorate have a natural appreciation of both. Ornaments and patterns, logos and images, can be designed and made. Symbols are different: they don't belong to anyone: they resonate: they are not so much designed as discovered.

People can perfectly well acquire the skill to decorate on their own, but it takes time and involves a good deal of waste and disappointment. Being difficult to describe in words, the necessary technical knowledge is usually absorbed by working alongside someone who has already mastered it. In tin-glaze (maiolica) painting, for instance, the

DECORATION

thickness of the glaze is crucial and one gets it wrong ten times before getting it right. Piccolpasso said it should be the thickness of a kidskin glove. That may have been perfectly clear when he wrote it in 1557, but to be shown would have been clearer still.

Then, assuming the glaze is right, what materials make colours and how are they prepared? Piccolpasso's treatise describes how these things were in his day and much of it still applies. Even though we can now buy a wide range of ready-made pigments, most potters' best colours are the ones they have prepared themselves by trial and error. Then again, how thick or thin should one paint? In practice there is an ideal range of thicknesses for every colour and one only learns it by trying and by seeing how the piece fires in the kiln. The same applies equally to every other form of ceramic decoration. Again, a painter's brushes, like a carpenter's tools, all have particular uses, and one has to discover what they can do and how to think and feel with them, rather as a musician thinks and feels with an instrument.

Each person's approach to decoration is only one amongst innumerable possible approaches that can all be valuable and convincing. Matthias Ostermann, in Montreal, uses materials very similar to my own but he works and thinks completely differently and I am amazed to watch him in action. The way he does it looks all wrong, but it works, and he achieves something I myself could never have done. In the last century, Owen Jones, William Morris and other distinguished artists used to speak of the Principles of Design. They were convinced that there were fundamental laws that had to be understood, practised and perfected before anything worth while could be reached. Within their canons of judgement it was true, but before long it became clear that certain impulses lying right outside their way of thinking could work equally well and within a couple of generations the main Principle was that there are no Principles. "There is no path to follow: your own footsteps make the pathway as you go."[9] I don't believe there is any 'right' way to decorate. Every field of action generates its own rules, but they are not absolute principles and the hitherto unimaginable can at any moment be discovered beyond them.

It is true that porcelain, stoneware, tin-glaze, slipware, enamel and lustre all have their peculiar technical disciplines, and each of them involves particular ways of thinking. Porcelain cannot be treated like maiolica: the bite of the colours is completely different and besides, porcelain forms and the hardness and delicacy of the material itself constitute almost another language. But someone may at any time interpret that language in ways never discovered before.

Generally speaking, my own decoration on tin-glaze earthenware begins with the making of the clay forms. I see the decoration and the underlying form as belonging to each other, as equally important aspects of a complete and unified vessel and I try to foresee the possible character of the decoration in advance, while my hands are deep in the clay. All kinds of things are possible; the decoration may be based on a geometric structure, it may be cursive and rhythmical, arresting or calm, colourful or quiet, or it may incorporate images. It depends a good deal on what the vessel is; as a rule a plate or a small bowl will take their place in a table-setting and work best if the design is calm and not too obtrusive. At one time we produced some plates decorated with a bold brush design in a beautiful chestnut colour. One day I saw someone lunching off one of these plates. The well-grilled sausages were so like the decoration that he had difficulty in identifying them. I understood then why the conventional blue and white has so long been in demand. One can see at a glance whether it is clean and it is easy to tell which is the food. The problem does not arise in the case of larger vessels intended to stand alone; they are relatively free from such tedious considerations.

When one is at the beginning, the making of clay forms and the process of decorating seem to be quite separate, but over a period of time they come closer and closer together in the mind's eye. The form and the texture, the ripple of the throwing, the undercuts and other articulations all begin to work as one.

When I am working completely freely a beckoning dream of an ideal reappears indistinctly again and again somewhere in the back of my mind. It is a kind of asymmetrical dance, a sequence of chasing rhythms and forms moving inwards, outwards and around in relation to an undefined centre that is implied everywhere but never seen. An inclusive unity. Something like it occurs when leaves are whirled by the wind: their movement is unpredictable, always changing, always coherent and dynamic although it has no logical structure or visible support. It did not occur to me at first, but I see now that the whole idea of this decoration refers back to the very beginning, when the pot was still soft clay being shaped on the wheel, its sides rising and spreading out from the motionless point in the centre. Thus the shape-making, which is the first process, and the decoration, which is the last, are finally unified by their relation to the invisible centre. Maybe I shall never capture this dream, but it still calls unexpected things up from the deep.

Meanwhile I decorate many pots in ways that are approximations to this idea, some that vaguely derive from it, and others that are quite different because in their case the idea would be inappropriate. In fact the dream has only appeared as a result of deco-

DECORATION

rating relatively simple things over and over again. This repetitive work led in the course of time to a better understanding of pigments and brushes and to a certain skill of hand that eventually made it possible to think wider. I believe that everyone has an equivalent concept somewhere in the back of their mind and one day it will become clear to them.

In the meantime, the regular work of decorating goes ahead. It is part of the workshop system and all of us, with varying levels of experience, are in it together, learning, sharing and reconsidering.

Each member of the workshop usually decorates what they themselves have made, beginning by following an existing design from a finished example. This shows which brushes are used and how the composition works on the round, which is difficult to tell from a drawing or a photograph. Some teachers regard the very idea of following a pre-existing design as an insult, but it can be a valuable stage in a process of development. Weeks may be spent trying to get it right, and then all of a sudden it arrives. It is a wonderful feeling, which we familiarly call 'lift-off'.

The regular workshop designs are decorative and unpretentious. People gain confidence by learning to do them. They have a strong character, but they are not personal and they have to be transmissible. People can only work together as a team if each one can enjoy what they are making and come to know the distinct character of each design as if it were their own. In a sense it becomes theirs as they work on it. With his own team of craftsmen in mind, William Morris vividly conveyed the idea of transmissible decoration in a lecture given over a hundred years ago:

> Something that will not drive us either into unrest or into callousness; something which reminds us of life beyond itself, and which has the impress of human imagination strong on it; and something which can be done by a great many people without too much difficulty and with pleasure.[10]

Such designs provide a way in, an entry for people who would otherwise not be sure how to begin, and who will in due course find ways of their own. One such was my assistant Suzanne, who once stood for half an hour gazing at a white, virgin pot, wondering what to do, until a gob of colour dripped from her brush and ruined it. When she had a finished example to follow, however, she went ahead with total enthusiasm. There is no shame in taking someone else's work as a starting point if one admires it. This has been happening since making began. Something else will grow from it. Whether one wishes it or not, it will change.

Everyone can sympathise with Suzanne's predicament. Some days one casts around for inspiration and feels completely lost. At other times a flood of ideas arrives unexpectedly, all coming at once, tripping over each other. It is a highly unprofessional state of affairs, but a common experience. When an idea arrives it is like a bird alighting on a branch. You can't force it.

So far as I am concerned, designs seldom start visually. I vaguely foresee their general character as a concept or an atmosphere with certain colours predominating. Intuitive trial brush strokes on a piece of newspaper sooner or later lead to a series of movements and motifs that fit the mood. I play with them and begin to see how they could work on the curved surface of the pot. Even a simple design is a system of forms, movements and relationships and they need to be resolved. At this stage one can sketch out possible placings and rhythms with dye to see how they will interact with the form. This can be done very freely since the dye burns away in the firing, but it is important not to spend too long on it. One needs to begin the real thing while the feeling is strong, not thinking it out too much in advance, or the sense of discovery is lost. I think there always has to be some emotional key or meaning behind the design. Simply trying to be decorative seldom gets anywhere. Lasting and satisfying decoration comes out of deeper ground.

If I am casting around for a starting point I often return to the letters of the alphabet in various forms, direct, or as mirror-images, inverted, paired, and so on. Letters of all cultures, Roman, Greek, Arabic, Hindi, Chinese, or whatever, are a meeting point between abstract forms and mental concepts. Our western letters O and Y and S, provide an example. O contains, encloses, imprisons, protects. Y rises, divides and opens: it invites, and it is like a chalice waiting to be filled. S is quite different; it can't contain anything; it slides like a snake; it connects two points by taking a long route between them; it curls but does not hold anything; it is on a journey. S is all mobile; O is stable. The letters T and X can be explored similarly. T rises up and it's no accident that Tree begins with it. But like a tree it has a top; from there it looks down and there is space underneath. X is an intersection, a meeting point, but it also looks outward, explores. It is very strong. And what about the strange letter G and my own letter, the beautiful A? The letter-forms work upon the intuitive mind, uniting abstract thought and sensory experience. Yet they remain some of the simplest of marks, each one distinct and unmistakable. Having played with them, one may in the end leave the letters behind; sometimes they lead on to something completely different, but they have provided a way to start imagining.

This is not to suggest that a decoration or an abstract mark is trying to convey a message in code. It's much simpler and more direct. Gombrich showed once and for all that signs and symbols are seldom precisely 'readable' and that the way people interpret them varies from age to age and place to place. If the maker's conception of a design is not picked up by anyone else, that doesn't greatly matter, though in fact it very often is. At the least it gives the decoration consistency; the eye and the mind play with it, extend movements, fill voids, imagine worlds within it. Samuel Palmer said that a painting is 'something between a thing and a thought'. It is equally true of good decoration.

Some years ago in Bangkok I acquired a small bowl made in Northern China during the early Sung dynasty. The decoration is a series of curved lines incised into the clay alternating with fine lines made with a small toothed instrument, under a satin-surfaced off-white glaze. Long afterwards I suddenly realised that the incised decoration is about clouds and rain, and, of course, it is a drinking-bowl and that is why the rim turns invitingly outwards. This dawned on me in the same way that one suddenly grasps the meaning of a line of poetry learnt by heart long ago. The shapes and colours in pottery decoration often suddenly appear completely afresh in this way, with a particular 'key' or meaning. But this only happens if the maker had a point of reference when the work was being done, an internal sense of order. Whether it is abstract or figurative, good decoration holds energy and communicates it. Decoration that comes only from undirected skill of hand has no secrets to offer. As Gombrich says, 'the exploitation of surprise is not the same as the grasp of a system of relationships', while random doodling offers only what he calls 'the discomfort of visual disorder'.

The Joseph Flower punchbowl, 1743. (Ashmolean Museum, Oxford).

24

BORROWING

It has to be faced, our latest exhibition in Edinburgh was not a success. The gallery people put it down to the weather, to the economic crisis, to the Easter holidays, etc. etc. and they think that it's partly the fault of the colour photograph on the invitation, – flames bursting from logs in the firebox and spiralling into the kiln. We used it because for a group show it didn't seem suitable to show any one person's work on the card. The gallery people now say that it would have been better to show something from the exhibition to indicate what people were actually going to see, but I don't think it would have made any difference.

The real explanation is that group exhibitions are notoriously difficult. People go for a name. In P.R. terms a group doesn't cut any ice. I knew this, but I don't regret trying a group show once again. It's a chance for each person to follow up their own ideas and work outside the normal repertoire. At the least it's a good safety-valve; one of the potters once said it was to show me where to get off. At the best it brings hidden talent to the surface; people discover new things and the younger ones begin to get their name before the public.

Perhaps it's asking too much. It's nice to assume that everyone has a marvellous store of ideas and that once you remove the stopper the genie comes out of the bottle. It does sometimes happen, but it's rare. Unfortunately not everyone has ideas that are both new and valid, and those who have probably need a lot more time to develop them.

Anyway, for one reason or another the potters seemed unsure of themselves. Some did variations on the kind of work they already knew, and others simply borrowed from elsewhere. One did variations on pre-Columbian Indian symbols, and I was dismayed to see someone else copying Chinese flower-designs straight out of a book.

Another adapted images from medieval manuscript illuminations, and another went back to Twenties Art Deco. It was all good fun, but they just weren't being themselves. It was a pity, because once people start borrowing they lose touch with their own inventive talent, and strong sources like these simply take over. The work feels new because it's unfamiliar, but it isn't new at all. It's only a shadow of someone else's invention.

I don't think there's anything wrong with borrowing; very few things in any art are completely original, and this is particularly true in ceramics, which has for two thousand years and more taken ideas from metalwork, fabrics, paintings, architecture and other sources, greatly enriching the art in the process. But it seems to me that borrowed ideas can only be put to good effect when a place has been made ready for them. They have to be re-interpreted to make sense in the new context, otherwise all that happens is simply mimicry.

Ceramics can mimic almost anything, clay and glaze are so versatile; the result may be profitable merchandise, but it counts for little in the long life of the art. Potters of the past manufactured merchandise and everyone knew what it ought to be like. Change usually came gradually, and the makers had time to absorb new ideas and adjust to new techniques. It is quite different today when everything happens very fast and illustrated books and periodicals abound, together with videos, TV programmes, exhibitions, and of course the great museum collections too. So many, many ideas to digest, objects to sketch, and designs to photocopy. It's hardly surprising that people get a creative colic when there's so much to take in; hardly surprising either that they are seduced into borrowing since many of these ideas have already been worked out, the mood established, the decisions already made.

The more people are given, however, the more they stand to lose. Before about 1500, Italian maiolica painters used to do delightful free-drawn designs of human figures and animals, full of fun and vitality, but when prints from wood-blocks and engravings became available they began to borrow. When they tried to imitate Raphael and Mantegna they lost their own inventiveness, and the next generation lost even the ability to copy well

When Louise was in Nepal she tried to get the pottery decorators to work out some new designs. "The trouble was," she said, "they simply copied each other. They love copying; that's the way they think."

It is understandable. Copying is enjoyable and relaxed because you can't lose your way. Besides, it's natural. Haven't human beings always imitated what they admire?

BORROWING

Imitation is an instinctive way of learning something new. We do it continually as we grow up, and we don't lose the habit simply by becoming adults. But constructive imitation and imitation from weakness are completely different. When one wishes to borrow, I think it is best not to work directly from the original but only from what one remembers. The most important things stay and the rest slips away. This is a natural and practical way of responding without being bound by literal detail, and it has been going on all over the world for centuries. Like a game of Chinese whispers, it may lead to nonsense, but sometimes it becomes more interesting than the original starting point, like the Celtic coins that were found here in a field last year, so vital and dramatic compared with the Roman stereotypes they were derived from.

The difficulties arise when there's a definite image in front of you. Memory is alive; it is selective; but a definite image imposes itself. This is often a problem today, when books and reproductions abound. One of the most influential of all is actually quite old: Owen Jones's famous *Grammar of Ornament*, published in 1856.[11] It shows thousands of patterns and symbols from all over the world, from Greece, Egypt, China to the 'ornament of savage tribes', a treasury of designs. Owen Jones knew the practical snags. He never meant his work to be a copy-book of ready-made designs. In Proposition no. 36 he says 'The principles discoverable in the works of the past belong to us; not so the results. It is taking the end for the means'. Which of course is the reverse of what happened. In effect, ornament borrowed straight from his book turns up in Victorian churches and civic buildings, apotropaic Greek and Pharonic symbols alongside lecterns and pulpits and 'ornament from savage tribes' in municipal offices. It was inevitable. A draughtsman employed to come up with a finished scheme could hardly be blamed for cribbing. Owen Jones himself knew that there is a deep divide between borrowing and re-creating, but the man in the drawing office had to produce results and time is money.

Had he taken time to look more closely he might have been highly confused. The designs in Owen Jones's book are not just ingenious ornaments; most of them have long, long histories; many different ways of thinking, feeling and imagining are implicit in them. As you explore them they work on you from inside. They get under the skin and into the brain. And it's not only ancient designs that do this. The same is true of any real artistic expression, ancient or modern. It has power. It's not a passive object of our curiosity or appreciation: we are being changed by it it as we take it in.

Not long ago I shared an exhibition with the tapestry-artist Tadek Beutlich, and during the preparations I asked if he had seen a certain exhibition that I thought he would have enjoyed. He said he hadn't dared to. He would have lost his way. Sometimes, he said, it took him ages to get back into his own work after seeing exhibitions and he couldn't afford the risk. I understood, but I was surprised that such a dynamic, innovative artist could be so vulnerable.

If Tadek and I react like this, is it surprising that students often show symptoms of indigestion? Colleges of art have an ambivalent role; they want to promote originality and at the same time they want their students to absorb the contemporary scene and the legacy of the past. The two objectives don't always mix. I think that is why the official curriculum often leads to satirical pastiche, which is a disguised form of mimicry, while at the same time it generates a popular iconoclastic movement. Feeling the power of the masters of the past, some students react against them, wanting their own work to be exclusively of the present and to emerge from their own unprocessed responses. One of the causes behind this understandable and somewhat bloody-minded attitude is the multitude of works of art that are now more accessible than ever before. And the reaction has a point. A child has a natural desire to imitate, but it also has a natural desire to find out for itself. As my small grandson called out to me this morning, "Don't show me. Let me do it!" And sometimes it works.

Richard Long said it very clearly in connection with his remarkable exhibition *Walking in Circles*, voicing a feeling shared by many people of his generation and the next.

> I think all my works, my actions, have no meaning outside what they are. So, if you think it's significant, then it's significant. All I'm saying is I'm just putting that stone on the ground, though obviously I realise it's never as simple as that. But my works should be completely self-contained, they shouldn't need any explanations or references, they should be things or ideas in their own right. They should have a life of their own and take their chances.[12]

That was an inspired and unforgettable exhibition, but it was like a symphony for one cello. And for all its austere originality, Richard Long's work has now, like many other new beginnings, itself become a convention with numerous followers. Nor was it really quite self-contained. It made this strong impact on us partly because in the back of our minds we were aware of what it was not, just as a silence is only sensed because of the sounds that preceded it.

It seems to me that borrowing and isolationism are both of them reactions to the bewildering variety of artistic impressions current in modern societies, and that both are unsatisfactory. Of course people can borrow; of course they can isolate themselves. Most creative people do a little of each. But above all what is needed is a focal point of conviction. It's not about art; it's about life. There's no recipe, but once it takes effect everything begins to fall into place. All that ever made a strong impression is still there, and whatever is needed will surface without being summoned and take on a new and unexpected form. Later it will have to be worked on, and it's only then that selection, comparison and the 'principles of design' come into play. Only then are they really about something.

In the museum of popular art at Belém near Lisbon is a small, abstract panel painted about a hundred years ago by a peasant, an attempt to describe a vision. I doubt if he or anyone else fully understood it, but you have no doubt when you see it that you are in the presence of something dynamic. It deals with a fact of life, like love, fear, awe or danger, a unique experience but not an isolated one. I think a god visiting the earth would pick out that panel immediately.

The peasant made a grand, pathetic effort. He used a piece of wood from a cattle-pen and the colours they kept for the farm carts. Given greater technical competence and better materials, what might he not have done? He would have longed for even a fraction of the facilities now available to every student in the Western world, but he had something of greater price, and many people today would give a lot for the commanding power of his inspiration.

25

PATRONAGE

I learnt yesterday that one of the potters, a talented girl in her mid-twenties, has applied for a grant to study the technology of ceramic lustre. It's sad news; we're all going to miss her lively presence and it puts us on the spot. Without her, there's bound to be a serious gap in our output. My team of potters has an almost perfect balance at present; everyone is near the peak of their training and it looked as if we could now tackle some new projects as well as producing a flow of pots of real quality.

It's her choice. She has the right abilities for a research project and in the long run she may do better that way than by trying to live by what she makes. Perhaps an academic environment has a special appeal because she has had a long dose of down-to-earth, practical work and it's nice to dream of having time to study and plan experiments. Besides, the Pottery is a cool place in winter and a laboratory with computer-controlled heating is a tempting alternative.

All the same, I can't help having doubts about this research. Reduced lustre is an untidy technique that depends as much on touch and techniques of firing as on knowledge of ceramic chemistry, because it concerns the partial combination of two indeterminate surfaces in variable conditions. It is far less predictable than the chemistry of glazes. The last potter I knew who tackled it gave up with a nervous breakdown.

I think the real reason behind her plan is self doubt – doubts above all about her ability to survive as a designer-maker in these competitive, inflationary times. She would not wish to go on working here indefinitely and sooner or later she would have to survive on her own.

These are not easy times for designer-makers. To prosper, you need a guiding star, determination, good health, and physical energy. You've got to care enough about making things to counterbalance the stress of paying your way. The romantic era is over and gone; costs and overheads, insurance and safety regulations are a serious business today. Talent and enthusiasm have to be backed up by P.R. and financial acumen. Every day, some young would-be artist has to decide whether to go professional or find other work and take the stand that Robbie Burns took, "I'll be damn'd if I ever write for money."

"Put the idea out of your mind", said Bernard Leach when I said I was thinking of becoming a potter. It surprised me; he seemed to be contradicting his own convictions. Later I saw that he was right: if you can forget the idea it's best to do so. Those who can't will go ahead anyway and take the consequences.

Until recently the consequences were unforgiving and our society is dotted with makers who lowered the flag when hope or health or resources gave out. More support is available today than even ten years ago, bursaries and loans, awards from sponsored competitions, grants for equipment and development of design and technology, as well as advisory services and commissioning agencies. Even so, it is a minute total compared with what is required by the performing arts, music and the theatre. Most of the support, however, refers to individuals, and in the nature of things it provides temporary opportunities, not long-term assurance and little of it is available to people working as a group. For the latter, the problem is not simply a matter of establishing a product, it's also a matter of sustaining it, year by year, and developing from it. Trade is one thing; creative growth is another, and it is often difficult to keep them going hand in hand. This is where patronage could be creative and important.

A great deal of the art we enjoy today came about because one person, perhaps centuries ago, saw certain possibilities where other people saw none. Patronage is first and foremost an act of imagination. For some, like Suleyman the Magnificent and Dr Barnes, it was a consuming passion. Sadly, it is currently more often regarded as a social duty. The 'One per cent for art' in present day building contracts is an attempt to introduce it on a public scale. It isn't always successful, but it has already brought about many works which have a significance far beyond the locations for which they were originally made.

There are really two kinds of patronage. One kind is extended to a business as a going concern and either supports it or better still extends its capabilities, like the big pot commission we did for the Chapman Taylor Partnership. The other is financial support that provides a breathing space for the development of equipment or ideas or other resources that could not have been achieved in normal trading conditions. A kind of development

Potter's sign, originally in the outer wall of a workshop at Velka Levaré, Slovakia, 1732. The potter is showing his work to a patron in riding clothes, who is paying him. Above is a traditional block wheel. The spear-like objects on either side of the fly wheel are tools for trimming, shaping and measuring. The vase of flowers and the birds signify well-being. (Museum of Applied Arts, Budapest).

PATRONAGE

capital, in fact, except that it isn't necessarily a single injection of capital: it could equally well, and perhaps better, take the form of guaranteed financial support over a certain period of time.

I think this latter possibility is positive and practical and its benefits all round could be much more widely recognised than they are at present. When a large company established its headquarters here after moving out of London a few years ago it seemed an auspicious moment to try it out.

I wrote to the Chairman mentioning how some of the most worthwhile works of the past had been made possible by patronage. Sometimes it took the form of financial support for a specific project. Sometimes it was patronage extended to a person or group, sustained over a certain period of time, to enable the artists to evolve techniques or ideas, take risks and undertake long-term projects that would not otherwise have been possible. In return the patron would receive a selection from the best of each year's work and certain things were occasionally made specially for him. His patronage received acknowledgement in displays and public events and in published, written material. Sums that are modest in terms of a large business corporation could prove a turning-point in the life of an atelier.

The response was lukewarm. The company had recently completed a multi-million pound new headquarters in an extensive park with a beautiful lake and the Chairman explained that any further expenditure had to be carefully monitored. As things turned out, they got into trading difficulties because of changes in international tariffs and moved their offices to a smaller site, so nothing came of the idea. In a number of cases, however, something on these lines is actually working. It costs the companies concerned a minute fraction of their annual promotional expenditure and vastly increases the scope and confidence of the studios receiving the support. It is far better than a one-off award or a temporary grant from a government-funded organisation because it enables the makers to plan for several years ahead.

This kind of arrangement is a positive step, modest though it is in comparison with the tremendous effect of patronage in ages past. It has considerable possibilities, especially when the persons most immediately concerned establish a cordial respect. Patronage can be an imaginative, innovative partnership, as I know from direct experience. It is by no means just a deal between the one who pays and the one who produces. That is only the lowest common denominator of patronage and all too often it ends in disappointment all round, which is how Johnson reached his definition of the patron as "a wretch who supports with insolence and is paid with flattery." Johnson, of course, had some famously unfortunate experiences.

> The notice which you [Lord Chesterield] have been pleased to take of my labours, had it been early, had been kind; but it has been delayed till I am indifferent, and cannot enjoy it; till I am solitary, and cannot impart it; till I am known, and do not want it.[13]

Personal patronage based on mutual understanding, however, can be satisfying to all concerned and highly enjoyable into the bargain, like the friendship between Turner and his patron, the Yorkshire squire Walter Fawkes.

An old friend of ours, who is himself an active patron of painters and musicians to the limit of his means, says that patronage has to be personal, there is no other way. "Public bodies can support institutions", he says, "but the patronage of art has to be from person to person. It comes from the incandescent vision of an individual. One must believe in the artist and take risks."

There was a good deal of sense in what he said, and this is why even the best intentioned public policies today tend to fall short. The "incandescent vision" is all too often missing and in its absence establishment support tends to be gathered up mostly by those who are best at applying for it. Real patronage is a creative relationship. It is difficult for institutions to establish such a bond, but individuals can do it spontaneously. The individual patron can inform, inspire and challenge an artist's imagination as well as providing material support over a period of time, but it needs patience and trust and insight, as well as an informed love of the art itself. If that is lacking, patronage seldom works. Once Sibelius was awarded a state pension he stopped composing.

It is said that Lorenzo de' Medici, on seeing a drawing by the thirteen-year-old Michelangelo, cried out in astonishment "This boy knows more than I do!" The tale makes a serious point. In the fullest form of patronage, material support is not the most important element, however much it may be needed. What matters even more is the patron's discernment and time and energy, and Lorenzo de' Medici understood it very well. Patronage itself is an art.

My own best patron is a man who has an uncanny way of sensing when some new impulse is needed and of guessing almost telepathically what it should be. He has no notable wealth or public influence, but he has always bought when I needed money and had good work to sell and he has the ability to see not only what things are, but what they could be. He has kept me abreast of publications and exhibitions and other events when I was too busy to know about them. We have travelled together and seen places I shall never forget and met unexpected people who opened my eyes. He has challenged me when I was cocksure and helped me to walk tall when I was down. Above all, he has the gift of drawing out ideas and energy I didn't know I had and of helping me to see that the universe is the best possible place to be in. Which of us, then, is the real maker?

One of the marks of his patronage was that it never appeared to be anything of the sort. It was always about something, always specific, and it mattered as much to him as to me. This is perhaps the secret of all the great patrons over the centuries, whatever their position in the world: they are following their star every bit as much as their artists. They have to.

One of the greatest of all patrons was Suger, Abbot of St Denis, whose construction of the new Abbey Church in the early twelfth century introduced the Gothic style to Christendom. Despite the demands made upon him by Church and State affairs, his personal commitment was immense and is unforgettably recorded in his book, describing what was done under his administration[14]. There, certainly, was an incandescent vision if ever there was one. He brought together the work of many kinds of artists and craftsmen in one supreme creative achievement which none of them alone could ever have imagined.

People often lament that direct patronage is no longer possible because the twentieth century cannot match the vast family fortunes of ages past. That is not true: the wealth exists, but it is impotent without vision and knowledge and love. Abbot Suger had no personal fortune; he was the son of a peasant.

Tin mine, St. Agnes, Cornwall.

26

TIN

In our plastic-package culture all kinds of materials can be obtained by ordering from a catalogue and put to use simply by following a recipe book. There is no need to know anything beyond their reference numbers, but even a little knowledge about a material means that it will be used with more respect, and therefore more economically as well. For that reason alone it is worth learning something about it. But it is also rewarding for its own sake, as I discovered in connection with tin. Originally I knew next to nothing about it except that it accounted for a large slice of my expenditure.

Because tin was used in the manufacture of tin cans its name is mistakenly associated with cheapness. It is in fact uncommon and quite valuable and tin cans have for many years been coated with other materials to save expense. Though tin sounds familar, few people have ever held a piece of this heavy, soft, silvery-white metal in their hands, since it is used mostly in metal alloys and is seldom seen in its pure form. The Incas knew it, and an artefact of pure tin has been found at Macchu Picchu; the ancient Egyptians used it occasionally, and of course the Greeks were familiar with it as an ingredient of bronze, though they were not sure where it came from. Herodotus wrote that it was found off the far north-west coast of Europe in the Cassiterides or 'tin-islands', *kassiteros* being the Greek word for tin. I think this half-legendary name must have referred to the Scilly Isles. Although they do not have any tin, Phoenician seamen would have had to pass them to reach Cornwall, which was the only source of the metal known to the ancient world in the Bronze Age.

Those traders obtained tin from the mineral cassiterite, dioxide of tin, which occurs as black, shining granules bedded in granite. The mineral was formed in the molten core of the ancient volcanoes that once towered as high as the Alps over what is now Cornwall and which were in the course of time eroded down to their stumps, exposing the rock in which the heavy metals solidified millions of years before. In Phoenician times cassiterite was found in the surface rocks, but miners of later ages had to go deeper and deeper to reach it. The legend that the young Jesus accompanied his uncle Joseph of Arimathea to Britain derives from the idea that Joseph traded in tin, which would have been blended with copper from Cyprus to make bronze.

Tin is very soft. The Lapps use tin-thread for embroidery. If a piece of the metal is bent it emits a strangely human sound known as the 'tin-scream'. It melts at only 232°C., which means that the molten metal can be strained through a cloth, as Piccolpasso recommended. At low temperatures, however, it disintegrates into powder, as is well known to musicians in cold climates, since organ pipes consist mainly of tin. Arab alchemists found that tin oxide makes glass and ceramic glazes white and the European pottery known as maiolica, faience and delftware derives from this discovery. This, of course, is why tin is of interest to us. The glazes we use for lustre and other colours contain about ten percent of tin oxide, which becomes white when it is finely ground. The particles are suspended in the fired glaze like a mass of microscopic snowflakes, making a beautiful ground for the colours. In short, tin has a remarkable history and wonderful properties, and it intrigued me even before I found the dark, sparkling cassiterite for myself, glinting in the granite on the site of a disused mine on Bodmin Moor.

Thus it was that one day I wrote from the Pottery to the manager of the Geevor tin-mine at Trewellard, asking for permission to make a visit. He sent a welcoming response and asked me to appear at the gate at 6.30 in the morning on January 7th.

The coast at Geevor is too exposed and rugged for any anchorage, so in time past the tin-ore was carried by pack-ponies twenty miles over the hills to St. Ives, where it was tranferred into ships and taken away for smelting. The old pony track is still quite distinct for much of the distance, and since I was going to St. Ives shortly before to celebrate Bernard Leach's eightieth birthday, it seemed a good idea to go on foot over the hills.

Walking in Cornwall in January is delightful; there is hardly anyone about and the hills have a powerful atmosphere. Having booked a room at the inn at Trewellard, near the mine, I started from St. Ives soon after sunrise, leaving the road by a farm track just outside the town and heading out across farmland. After a few fields of cattle the ground rose abruptly and I was soon catching my breath on the steep, open slopes dotted with furze that lead to the Amalveor hills. Looking back from the ridge the deep indentations of the Cornish coast stretched far away to the east and the sun caught the horizon line of the open sea. What awe-inspiring space! Ahead of me lay the downland, bleak, tawny-brown with dead bracken and tussock grass, bordered on the north by tors facing across the sea towards Ireland.

I soon picked up the pony track, rutted by sheep-walks and pitted with their footprints, and followed it westwards. It was marvellous cold, grey, winter weather with a mild breeze, low cloud and flurries of light rain, the kind of weather that looks dreadful from indoors but is delightful if you are out and about. Inspired by Basho's book *The Narrow Road to the Far North*, which was in my pocket, I composed *haikus* about things that specially caught my attention.

It was so splendid up there that after a few hours I made a detour to prolong the journey by going over to Carn Galver, a long, beaky tor with steep sides, rather like a ship rising out the mist, and I stopped there to eat some bread and cheese. Descending from the rocks, and then going up and down across several ridges in open ground, I was enveloped by ever-thickening mist and soon lost my bearings. The pony track must be a mile or two to the left, but the ground ahead rose up in a way not indicated by the map and I was now on a ridge of rocks that I hadn't noticed before the mist came down. It's extraordinary how quickly this kind of thing happens. On the far side of the ridge, pressing through dense, tall bracken, I rapidly got soaked from head to foot. The breeze dropped and from the right came the regular blasts of a muffled foghorn. The coast must be nearer than I had supposed. The best thing would be to take the downward slope to the left, which must eventually reach a stream and lead to some habitation. It seemed sense, but after an hour I arrived beside some recognisable rocks, and nearby appeared the very same swathe of bracken I had pushed through at the beginning. So much for making a descent. The foghorn now came from dead ahead, no longer from the right. The map was no help in this mist and it was getting dark.

Following the downward slope all the time, I came eventually to a stream which led in the end to a farm track. By now the mist had become a heavy drizzle and it was almost dark. The air cleared as the drizzle turned to rain, and through the darkness I saw the lights of a village in the distance. After another hour of squelchy walking I reached the outlying houses. Five minutes more and I was standing, dripping, in the lamplight outside the inn at Trewellard. I could hardly believe it, the landlady who greeted me was the very image of Sally, an exuberant girl who worked for me fifteen years ago. Before showing me my room she advised me take off my socks and trousers, a sensible if somewhat unusual welcome.

It was warm and bright and there was a smell of food. Before long I was sitting at table with beer and supper in front of me and a large bath towel around my middle, while my trousers dripped on a rack by the kitchen stove. Gradually the bar filled with friendly people, several of whom made humourous comments on my attire in such strong Cornish accents that I could only guess at some of the exchanges. I retired early to bed with Basho and the *haikus* to get dry. It had been an altogether splendid day.

Next morning Mr. Pascoe met me at the gates of the mine. He had planned my tour with thoughtful generosity, arranging for various people to show me their particular assignments, while he himself met me at intervals throughout the day to explain the general picture. I was dressed up again, this time in waterproof leggings and a miner's helmet, and soon we were going down one of the mine-shafts in an iron lift with a group of miners whose pleasantries, once again, I could barely follow, being richer Cornish than I had ever heard before. To me, it could almost as well have been Catalan. The lift stopped several times to drop the miners off at their different adits – horizontal passages leading off the lift shaft. It became distinctly warmer as we descended and by the time I got out to follow a lamplit tunnel to the rock-face I assumed we must be at the bottom of the mine. We were in fact only about half way down, seven hundred feet or so, but a world away from the open hillside of the previous day. The deepest adits, I learned later, were opened up during the first world war, thirteen hundred feet below the surface and extending half a mile out under the sea.

The mine, or rather the cluster of mines, had been worked more or less continuously since the days when the Phoenicians came, literally scraping the surface, and as the workings went deeper the whole hill became honeycombed with tunnels and caverns, many of which were never accurately recorded. It is extremely difficult to map the exact positions of underground excavations and in some mines the structural pillars left to support the roof were accidentally cut into too far, causing disastrous falls of millions of tons of rock. At Geevor the granite is so tough that such collapses never occurred, though even now the location of the older workings is still very uncertain.

The general principle today is that horizontal adits are driven from the main shafts at intervals of a hundred feet, following the lodes of tin-ore, which are at an incline of about 60°. When the adits reach their full practicable extent, traverses or sideways excavations are made, following the ore obliquely upwards until the next adit is reached, leaving columns of rock in position to support the roof of the cavern. When the blocks of tin-bearing granite are drilled and blasted free from the face they slide down the floor of the traverse and are caught by a stockade at its base. There they are split into smaller blocks and loaded into trucks that used to be pulled by ponies but are now drawn by small railway engines. The rock is taken to the main shaft where it is winched to the surface in a giant hopper. The blocks are then split by a heavy jaw-crusher; the valueless material is discarded and the ore-bearing rock is stage by stage broken into smaller and smaller fragments. Since the Cornish ores contain only around 3% cassiterite, an enormous amount of material is discarded. I don't know what they do with it all.

The fragments eventually become fine enough to be carried in a water-curtain over inclined magnetic screens, where the iron-containing particles are separated out. The cassiterite is eventually dried out as a fine grey powder which is stored for transportation in small sacks. Only when you try to lift one of these sacks do you realise how heavy the mineral is compared with the granite from which it has been separated. It was sacks like these that the pack ponies used to carry over the hills before road transport became available.

The entire operation is intensely hard, skilled work, especially the work at the rock-face, even though the equipment has been continuously modernised over many generations. The drilling and blasting of the rock takes place in hot, damp, confined spaces, and is potentially dangerous at every stage. In the days when pewter, about 80% tin, was in everyday use, and the mining was carried on with candles and hand-chisels, the labour and risk must have been extreme. One of the things that struck me was the total difference from life on the surface. No wonder that miners, like seamen, have always had a strong sense of solidarity. They depend for their survival on each other's courage and self-reliance, and they work in conditions that are almost unknown to people who live on the surface. They are different from other men and they are united by a unique bond of corporate self-respect.

There are not many sources of tin in the earth's surface, and naturally it has always been expensive. The Cornish mines were probably the earliest known of all because they were just within reach of the parts of the ancient world where tin was needed. In modern times they were overtaken by far richer mines in Bolivia and in the Urals and by alluvial deposits in Malaysia and Nigeria, but at the time of my visit, Cornwall still produced between 2-3% of the world output.

After the second world war the International Tin Council maintained the price-level by buying up all the tin coming on to the world market and releasing it at intervals to meet demand. This was meant to assure the producers of a good return on their outlay, but the high price had unfortunate effects. It forced many users of tin to find cheaper alternatives, and it also led to an increase in tin-production until eventually it exceeded the ITC's resources and they went bankrupt. Suddenly there was a surplus of tin on the world market and the price halved overnight. Mines working the lower grade ores were the first to go out of business and before long all the Cornish mines had to close. Geevor was the last to go. For the first time for centuries the hill is silent.

27

CREATION

I have just seen a magazine article which includes comments on one of our recent exhibitions. It's quite complimentary and it's enjoyable reading, until you come to the place where the pots are called 'creations'. This word is frequently used today in design and the applied arts and, to my ear, it always jars, especially when it is applied to our own work. It suggests that we are in supreme control, which is not true, and it's a denial of all the changes and chances that affect the pots along the way.

I suppose this use of the word comes from the world of fashion-design. A glamorous, elitist word like 'creations' is highly suitable for the presentation of a designer's new collection. It is good publicity, but it also has a sound, practical point, for it distinguishes things made under the designer's personal supervision from products that are passed on to manufacturers. A 'creation' suggests something unique, with the magic of the designer-maker's direct touch. Since it implies that whatever is so described has originated at the highest level it is also a popular commercial term. So much so that all sorts of things are now referred to as 'creations': clothes, lighting, cookery, carpets, kites, wedding cakes, flower arrangements, tapestries, childrens' toys, and so forth, and pots too.

I know it is being used appreciatively, but it is an awkward term to apply to pottery and ceramics. Potters re-combine and transform materials, giving them uses and meanings they didn't have before and their work may lead to designs and products made with some degree of art, but they are seldom if ever creations. The word 'creation' is best kept for works of the highest conceivable kind. Words, after all, are very much more than labels; they are tools for thinking with. If a key word is used wrongly we lose our bearings about our position in the scheme of things.

At one time, people used the simple word 'maker' to describe those who made

POTTERY, PEOPLE AND TIME

The Pharaoh Ramesses III being created on the potter's wheel by the gods Horus and Thoth: wall painting at Medinet Habu, Thebes, c.1180 B.C.

CREATION

anything, whatever the medium. The Greek word 'poet', which comes from a verb meaning 'to make' was used in the same way. They were matter-of-fact words, whereas 'creation', from the Latin 'creare', suggests the power to bring into existence not only a product but the idea as well and even the material itself. The word 'maker' used to be applied across the board, to architects and musicians and poets and equally to stone-masons, blacksmiths and potters. It expresses something they all share, and after long neglect it is now back in favour. This is happening because everyone has got sick of distinctions and differences: when, for instance, is an object art and when is it craftsmanship? What is the difference between art and design, between invention and originality, between ornament and symbol, between form and concept? The borderlines have become blurred, but the word 'maker' includes everyone.

In some ways, however, the word 'maker' is inconveniently broad. It doesn't distinguish between the act of making and the idea that guides it. From this point of view a stonemason and a poet, for instance, are poles apart. The mason works directly on the physical material and the way it is handled is a vital part of the art, whereas a poem takes shape in the mind and the way it is written down is relatively unimportant.

Fortunately, two key words make the distinction. The first is 'forming' and the second is 'inventing', which is currently used in a specialised way, but it comes from the Latin *invenire*, meaning simply 'to find'. Where a columnist of today might write 'creative', people in earlier times would have said 'inventive', meaning one who finds, and I think this would usually be more appropriate.

It's a more modest word and perhaps rightly so. Whatever is given form must have been potentially in existence beforehand. Thus the maker is one who finds or 'invents' forms that may never have been seen before but which always existed in the realm of possibilities. What is found depends partly on the capacity of the 'inventor' and partly on the natural formations of the universe reflected in number or form or sound or movement.

Newton wrote vividly about this. In his mathematics and his studies of the behaviour of light and of moving bodies he knew that he was disovering principles that had always been in existence, and he did so with humility. I think he would have been dismayed by the things that have been said on his behalf by succeeding generations. He was convinced that the physical principles he defined could only be properly understood in relation to a universal 'expanding force' whose nature he could not determine, though he spent years of his life trying to do so. A short time before his death he said,

> I do not know what I may appear to the world, but to myself I seem to have been only like a boy playing on the sea-shore, and diverting myself in now and then finding a smoother pebble or a prettier shell than ordinary, whilst the great ocean of truth lay all undiscovered before me.[15]

Most people, and probably all makers, have shared something of his emotion. They know that their ideas are not absolutely their own, but are brought about by some interchange between their minds and a source beyond their control. The mythology of the Muses was not merely a pious classical convention but a way of describing the experience of innumerable poets and musicians at times of inspiration. Others described it as a dream-vision, as Chaucer did, saying that a new poem came to him 'in swoon' from beyond himself.

This might be just a modest literary device, but I believe it has more to it, that it is an accurate way of describing how an idea took possession of him, since so many other makers have also attributed particular works to a visionary dream. Mozart, arrogant and 'touchy as gunpowder' in his social affairs, described in the famous 'Letter to a certain Baron' how his musical compositions arrived in his mind with a complete and 'given' quality that overawed him. And Van Gogh's letters to his brother Theo are those of a man continually finding and discovering and being precipitated into one new work after another with total conviction and utter humility.

Makers can often say how and where an inspiration came to them, but why it came and the form it took remains unaccountable. They can apply their skills in whatever way they choose, but the source of their ideas and their sometimes overwhelming motive power remains mysterious. Some are driven on relentlessly by the succession of ideas; others, like Wordsworth, find that the inspiration runs dry and they do not know how to get it back. Most makers depend for their livelihood on having new ideas, but there is no guarantee that any ideas at all will arrive next day. The maker can open the way for them and respond once they arrive, but no-one can determine what they will be like. Inspiration, or the 'right-brain experience' as it is often called today, operates through its own hidden laws. Keats, for one, was wary of his impulses, knowing that insight and hallucination, horror and ecstasy, are divided by a very fine line.

> ...Art thou not of the dreamer tribe?
> The poet and the dreamer are distinct, Diverse, sheer opposite, antipodes.
> The one pours out a balm upon the world. The other vexes it.[16]

Sori Yanagi tells a story of the brilliant Japanese woodblock artist Shiko Munakata.

CREATION

Once, at an exhibition, Munakata halted in front of one of his own works and exclaimed admiringly, in a loud voice, "Terrific! terrific!" When a bystander reminded him that he himself was the artist, he retorted "No – this was made by God; I disclaim all responsibility!" Yanagi comments, 'In talking of God here, he was almost certainly referring to the Buddha.... to that state of intellectual unawareness, that absence of any intrusive self, that represents a supreme ideal in Buddhism".[17]

All of which is very different from the contemporary jargon applied to artists and designers and their so-called creations, a jargon that did not originate amongst the makers themselves, but in the media and amongst promoters and salesmen.

"Jesus was the supreme artist", wrote Van Gogh to his brother Theo, "because for His material he took living people". And it was the supreme artist Himself who said

> The wind bloweth where it listeth, and thou hearest the sound thereof,
> but canst not tell whence it cometh, and whither it goeth... [18]

Wind, breath and Spirit are all translations of one and the same word, the word that occurs in the Creation poem at the beginning of the Book of Genesis, which has been translated as 'God sent a great wind to blow on the face of the waters'.

A child making something.

Every act of making, the delight, the compulsion, the anguish and the ecstasy, is a reverberation of the great wind. The desire to make is born again in every human child, which is perhaps one facet of what is meant by man being made in the image of God. But human beings can only work within the laws of nature governing them and the world around them. In time to come they will make things undreamed of today, but by themselves alone they cannot create anything. Nor can they claim what they make as their own in any personal sense, for behind all human making, whether we call it forming, finding, designing or inventing, is the great wind.

That, I believe, is why every act of dedicated making matters, great or small, whether in solid material or sound or number or words or knowledge. It connects the particular here-and-now with a breath of the wind that moved on the face of the waters at the beginning of time. Sometimes a maker becomes purely and simply a vehicle for this force. Then the process of making begins to become creative in the full sense of the word.

Aldous Huxley once said that Beethoven's last quartets were proof of the existence of God. His bland statement reaffirms what has been expressed again and again in many forms over the ages. Beethoven himself scrawled an invocation in the margin of the manuscript of the quartet opus 135: "Thou the best of all powers, the image of all wisdom, present throughout the world, thou sustainest all things".

On such a level as this the process of making resembles what scientists term 'an emergence', signifying a phenomenon with new properties that could never have been foreseen. Here the word 'Creation' really begins to mean something.

This seems a strangely high point to have reached after beginning a few pages back with a journalist's report on a pottery exhibition, but it is not irrelevant. Creation is a high word and it would be a shame to let it be devalued. If it is expended on things that are already known it cannot point beyond them.

28

WASTE

I'm a bit down. We've just had a bad firing, a very bad one, in the big wood-kiln, caused by violent winds and also by various alterations to the normal procedure, things that weren't explained to everyone in detail beforehand. They should have been obvious, but evidently they weren't. Anyway, it's gone wrong and weeks, no, months of work is wrecked. It's no good dwelling on it, but perhaps I can think myself out of the pain by unloading it on to paper.

To cap it all, it happened just after I'd given a talk in the Ashmolean Museum, ending with a tour of the Collection, handling some of the ceramics and giving appreciations of them. It was a wonderful day but now, remembering all we talked about, my own words come back to batter me. How dare I talk as if I understood anything? And oh those wonderful pots in their safe, shining showcases! How was anything so perfect ever made by men of feeble flesh and blood? Those potters seem never to have made mistakes. It's as if they never had to learn. The glazes always perfectly fused; the clay never split or pitted; the brushwork so unerring, the idea so absolutely right. It's a magical world, a mystery I can't enter. There's a locked door somewhere and I'm outside.

Not true, of course. They must have lived through dozens of failures to learn enough to be able to make these wonderful things. They must have done. Somehow the world must have absorbed a mass of bad shapes, badly made, badly glazed, badly painted, but goodness knows where they are now. Those things weren't really wasted, of course. They were going somewhere. The people were learning. The real waste came with the things that were made later, made perfectly, should have been beautiful, and were lost at the very last stage in the firing. Yes, you can find plenty of that, the real waste. It puts our losses in perspective just to think of it.

WASTE

I've seen a photograph of a valley in south-east China where tea-bowls were made in the Sung dynasty. For half a mile it's several feet deep with wasters. Three or four feet deep! Then at Fustat, where I've trodden the ground myself, the broken sherds and wasters go down ten feet or more below the surface. Centuries of waste. At Orvieto they built walls and houses from faulty jars and pitchers from the kilns, and here in England the town of Hanley is founded, quite literally, on wasters of early salt-glaze. The rules of the game don't change.

Archaeologists love to find wasters around old kilns. This is direct historical evidence. Potters regard it differently. We think of the time spent refining the material, working and making, carefully setting the kiln, sweating at the fire, the counting of the cost, the explanations and the blame, the 'Why oh why?' Every potter knows it, past, present and future. Shared troubles underlie the fellow-feeling between potters all the world over. Lost firings are not easily forgotten.

The hurt goes deep. You know the material through and through. That makes the loss harder to take, like a broken romance. The things that counted most were the fruit of many years, years of the moment-to-moment commitments required by every kind of art. Nothing signifies unless the maker gives something of himself, and loss or failure come in the same measure. The old tale of the Chinese potter who failed for the third time to achieve the red *sang-de-boeuf* glaze and dived into his own furnace, is close to the mark even today. Today we may have computerised kilns, but things still go wrong and human nature doesn't change. If sane people moan and wish to die when a few pieces of baked clay are lost, it can't be for the material itself, but because to their mind something elemental and true had been drawn into it. That's the real loss, not the time or the effort or the money.

The sense of waste is overwhelming and thoughts of annihilation follow it, storms, wrecks and pestilence. The mind broods on darkness and the destructive forces of the world from the beginning of time, crushing hope, obliterating beauty.....Gloom closes every door, slams it tight, until eventually it dies from its own excess. What is lost is after all only a matter of graven images and the hardest hurt is in the mind. Graven images. Artists have always been susceptible to them. They are found not only in the Old Testament but wherever anyone projects into material objects values that really belong to life itself. Whatever is lost was only the reflection of a reflection, certainly nothing to be bowed down to or worshipped by anyone with his wits about him. Haven't I understood even yet? If one can't bear losing, then one shouldn't gamble.

Yet the 'if-onlys' drag me back. If only the fuel had been drier, the setting more open, if only someone had seen the column leaning, if only someone had paid attention! If only I had thought! Too late now, too late to change, but still one has to compare what happened with what might have been. The circling anguish, repeating and repeating, is not just foolish regret, it's also a necessary attempt to understand what happened and why.

If only some magic could cancel the mistake. Can't the past be changed if you only wish it hard enough? But the facts can't be dodged by fictions or drink or sex or aggression. I have to face up to the situation, go into it and through it and out the other side, acknowledging my own fault. These regrets only take away the here-and-now, the light of the present, the only place where anything new begins.

Back to the Museum again, those noble forms, colours, glazes, dancing lines and designs all fused into a perfect, finished whole. It's all laid out before me, the ideas, the touch, the poetry, so close. What can't be on display is the time it took to learn, the trials of materials and tools, the inspiration for the designs, and the wastage along the way. The potters of past ages must have known it all. They lived and worked and prayed, made love and died, against a background of failures and wasted effort that seemed at the time like acts of a wanton god and turned out to be only their own misjudgement. Whoever tests their hard-earned and short-lived skills in the same materials today has to follow the same rules or quit.

29

THE VISIT

Answering Helmut's letter I wrote that he would be welcome, but I had some doubts. A party of day-release patients from a mental hospital in South London does not fit easily into a working day, but how could one refuse? Helmut had asked about a suitable place to picnic before the visit. Hoping it would not rain, I suggested the wildfowl park in the Thames water meadows just above Pangbourne. As things turned out it was a perfect May afternoon.

Helmut came straight in, proclaiming in a resolute German accent,

"It was a master-suggestion! We lunched under the trees and the lake was crowded with waterfowl from five continents; yes, there were also the black swans of Australia to celebrate our annual expedition. We are astounded by such beauty, and also we bring PRESENTS!"

He could not have been less like the stereotype of a psychiatric art-therapist. He looked more like a nightclub bouncer, a man in his fifties, of medium height, very broadly built, his face fringed with a short beard, and completely and smoothly baldheaded, like a cross between a teddy-bear and a well-stuffed German sausage. The charisma and the unflappable goodwill were plain, and his magnetism for the patients, to whom he was devoted. They drifted into the building after him, a collection of men and women mostly between twenty and forty years of age, accompanied by Helmut's Italian colleague Paula and George, the driver.

Several of our visitors were solemnly holding peacock feathers and the plumage of various other birds in front of their faces and presented them to us as a greeting. I did my best to welcome them, though it was difficult to meet anybody's eye and whatever I said sounded slightly fatuous, but the feathers were a brilliant beginning, as Helmut must have foreseen. Feathers kept turning up in unexpected places for years afterwards.

Helmut Muller, about 1986.

THE VISIT

Helmut made great play with introductions. By the time we finished everyone had shaken hands with everyone else several times over. The pantomime was important, passing time together and establishing, as far as possible, where and who we were. Then he strode over to where Julian was throwing at the wheel and a number of patients followed him as if carried along in the draught. Julian, always out-going and ready for anything, understood exactly what was required. He coned the clay rapidly up and down and opened it out into the form of a large pitcher. Then he did the old circus trick, making the pot wobble precariously on the verge of collapsing. Everyone was riveted. He righted it, drew it up, wired it off and showed it off on the board in front of him, all much faster than he would normally have done. Sighs of relief – or disappointment? The performance broke the ice and a little group remained beside the wheel for some time, perhaps half hoping that next time the pot would collapse.

Helmut spoke emphatically, half laughing, half solemn.

"See how the clay is alive! Too bad that our master-potter Thomas could not be with us today. He had a turn last night and struck his friend Godfrey, so instead of joining the party he is unfortunately in the padded room. He would have enjoyed this, wouldn't he Frank?"

The mention of the padded room surprised us. Was this a deliberate part of the therapy, or just Helmut being spontaneous? No-one seemed bothered. Frank grinned wistfully and gave me another tail-feather. I stuck the quill in a lump of clay and the feather waved elegantly in the draught.

"It looks good, doesn't it?"

"It's very soft," said Frank, meaning the clay, presumably, not the feather.

I was wondering how to give the visit some shape. We quite often showed student groups round the workshop, but this party was different. They had dabbled in pottery and clay-modelling as part of their therapy, but they weren't interested in the materials or the processes as such. They didn't ask anything or make any comments and stood around, expectant and listless, as if separated by invisible veils. Helmut's demonstrative enjoyment of everything helped to bridge the gap, but as the host I wanted somehow to back him up. It seemed best to follow the processes through, hoping that sooner or later some point of interest would arise.

"Now we look at Alan's big kiln," announced Helmut, "where the pots get their beautiful colours."

We proceeded through the rear workshop to the kiln, but many of the visitors were diverted by other things along the way. Helmut himself disappeared. The kiln aroused little interest. Had it been alive with flames it would have been a different matter. The patients responded to happenings much more than to things. When I located Helmut some time later he was talking animatedly to the potters Ursula and Mary about his portraits, as if nothing else in the world mattered.

"I form the structure of the head in black crayon, "he was saying, "a dynamic black, with stark lines and delicate lines proportionated to the sitter's character. The execution must be rapid because my subjects are unable to pay attention for long. Background jazz is a good standby. The real fun begins with the colour crayons. A face is not black or pink. Look carefully and you see it is a RAINBOW! When I pick up the colours I go half crazy."

On a subsequent visit we saw some of these portrait drawings, which were strong and highly accomplished. Just now, however, I was wishing he would pay more attention to the people who were wandering around the kiln. One of them was trying to use the heavy gas poker as a telescope and another was getting entangled in the wood-pile. George came quickly to the rescue. Meanwhile Helmut turned up and took charge of the poker.

"You should be careful with artists' equipment," said Helmut. "It's expensive."

The patient drifted over to Edgar's painting bench and offered him another peacock feather.

One of the best ways of making contact was by going over people's names once more and enquiring about their occupations, since most of them had jobs before being admitted to hospital. The answers were surprising: amongst others, there was a builder, an accountant, a panel-beater, an army officer, and a telephone engineer. All had been reduced by illness to shadows of the responsible men they once had been, but their knowledge and abilities seemed to be still intact. It was as if the main switch governing motivation and meaning had been turned off, and all that remained was a matter of passing the time. Helmut's forthright enjoyment of everything was an extraordinary contrast. He was now in the next room, forcefully addressing everyone within range.

"...they should have got the artist who does the posters for Tennants Strong Lager. Boy, he works in the tradition of a little known MASTER of French poster art called CASSANDRE. He had all the wit of PUNCH and each poster was on the level of Picasso... There is a whole series... I saw only one, a jazz trumpeter. The technique is sculptural. It must have been constructed with card in relief and then photographed... as if you were to cut out thin slabs of clay and form a face, body, arm or what have you by tucking the slabs over and under one another. Like this..." (he showed the idea)... "resulting in powerful REALISM. I mean, so far removed from IMITATION... The trumpet must have been created by flinging several cans, empty of course, on the main road for the traffic to go over...the can squashed in just the right way to express the trumpet was used for the final work."

He was carried away by the idea.

"When a Macdonald's box or a motorbike gauntlet is run into the tarmac by the London traffic... illusion of powerful relief results. Dürer would have looked on in despair if he put them beside the gothic folds of the Madonna's robe...I once found a traffic-compressed FAST-FOOD-BOX, sewed it with my hand-operated Singer on to cardboard and hung it in Art Therapy. It must still be there."

"There's a lot of art around, once you see it," someone commented.

"Art is transformation," concluded Helmut. "Now let us enjoy the art of the Pottery."

The group broke up and people wandered. It's amazing what an area fourteen patients can cover without apparently moving. Still, nothing had been broken and everyone appeared relaxed. We tried to catch their interest, wedging clay, pulling handles, showing them the painting and stamping of designs, and they responded after a fashion, though it was difficult to hold their attention for more than half a minute at a time. One couldn't interest them like ordinary visitors, but neither could they be entertained like children. All that seemed possible was to pass time together in a friendly fashion, emphasising anything involving change and movement that could focus the attention, however briefly, and help them to carry on. What else can people do but carry on? It takes courage. In physical distress the courage is often inspiringly clear; in mental distress it is less evident, but it is there just the same and it is needed every bit as much.

By now several people were becoming quite communicative about themselves and one or two brought out sketchbooks to show us their drawings, some of which were very accomplished.

Helmut interrupted us. "Gather round, everyone. Watch how Alan will make a pot for us." I had been expecting this and had some big lumps of clay ready.

"I want to touch the clay first," said one of the party. I held out the ball. He touched it and smiled conspiratorially at me. Several other people did the same, as if we were sharing a secret. Play-acting perhaps, but at least it was a kind of contact.

I centred the clay and drew up a tall form. One man gaped, motionless, as if sud-

POTTERY, PEOPLE AND TIME

denly turned to wax. Two others were disconcertingly on their hands and knees trying to look into the wooden casing of the electric motor. They looked crazy, and I was caught unawares when one of them asked

"Is it a variable resistance control?"

I nodded.

"I thought so. They're good, but the brushes wear out quickly."

"Try phosphor-bronze," said the other and winked at me. He tapped a ball of clay several times and drifted off. There wasn't time to interpret this gesture because the pot had to be completed. I formed a lip and applied a handle to make a better show. It wasn't a great pot, but at least it was a happening. How much does a happening count, if it's forgotten two minutes later? .... Or, come to that, twenty years later?

"Behold, dear friends," announced Helmut, "Alan has made for us a FORM. A form of great beauty. Look well – enjoy!"

The group was already dispersing, however. I gave up trying to organise anything and simply continued throwing on the wheel, doing it properly from now on, watched by the two people remaining from the group, and exchanging ocasional comments with them. The rest of our visitors seemed happy enough and most of them found something to watch or someone to talk with. When eventually I rose from the wheel Helmut was discoursing in the main workshop with Paula, two of the potters and two patients.

"In Liebermann's day the first Cezannes went on show," he was saying. "The critics accused him and other expressionists, sorry impressionists, of faulty vision, and since then scientists claim that most impressionists did indeed suffer from faulty vision... So it was said, Look at this boy in the waistcoat, his arm is far too long. And Liebermann replied, That arm is so beautifully painted it can't possibly be long enough..."

One of my group, an attractive woman in early middle-age, with a lilting Irish accent, was telling me about her childhood home in Sligo, where her grandfather discussed reincarnation with the poet Yeats. She didn't believe in it herself, she said, but her grandfather had lived many lives. Before we could get to the bottom of this, however, Helmut broke into the conversation with historical reminiscences of Hanau, his birthplace.

"...so they rounded up the good peasant lads and sold them to London. Arrangement, a good price for each lad and a better one when he was killed in action... So the Prince urged London to send his boys to the worst trouble spots of the developing British Empire..."

THE VISIT

Was this a recognised therapeutic technique? It was hard to believe. Helmut himself was not exactly normal. Well, who is? Yet if the point was to pass time agreeably, then he was a master, for wherever he went he created events, real or imaginary, with gripping detail.

"The Hessen regiments fought in the American War of Independence. One Christmas they were all pissed on hot toddy. Ursula is a potter from Germany. Ask her some time about Gluhwein or FEUERZANGENBOHLE – Recipe: large silver cup or special Alan vessel is filled with rare champagne and white wines. Fire-tongs are placed across the vast cup and a sugarloaf is fixed in the tongs and doused with good brandy and set alight and the sugar-brandy drops into the champagne making fireworks for background effect. Add herbs and fruit if you will.... Be that as it may, a U.S. general decides to attack the HAPPY HANAU HESSIANS and promptly secures a historic Christmas defeat. A fair cop... and in return the Hessians introduce the Christmas Tree to America..."

The fireworks theme led into a discussion about kilns. Could they construct a wood-fired kiln in the hospital precincts? It might be too unpredictable; as it was, the glazes behaved strangely enough in the gas kiln. Sometimes, George said, the ceramics had to be taken out with a hammer and chisel. Too true, said Helmut, "We do not employ all our materials as Alan would have us to do, but sometimes we ACHIEVE THE IMPOSSIBLE by other means. Diaghileff said to his dancers, Surprise me! Well, we have surprised many people, isn't it true, Henry? Henry, by the way, is Art Therapy's expert in surprises.

"Last Christmas..." grinned Henry, "with the crib."

"Ah, the Christmas crib... That was indeed an incident."

I was glad that a number of our visitors had wandered into the garden. The apple trees were in blossom and the sun was shining. It must surely be very therapeutic to stroll underneath them and cup the clusters of flowers in the hand, as several people were doing. Therapeutic for us too, since it relieved us from trying to devise another event.

"Wandering like the Wandle..." murmured Helmut reflectively, "our little Wandle, the river that gave Wandsworth its name. Did you know, the Wandle, which used to serve merely as a rubbish dump, like most of London now, has been cleaned up and banked to uncover its beauties. A large complex has been developed, run by the Camden Lock people backed up by Sainsbury's, where William Morris's art and craft printing works used to be. It will be workshops, studios, galleries, restaurant, pub, and what beautiful buildings too. Squat ground level design. ARCHES. Beautiful roofs and brick and flint masonry, and the river too – straight out of Gainsborough! A beautiful giant waterwheel restored to running order. It runs just the opposite way to what one expects; it has something to do with the way the water hits the paddles. The silent noise...standing on the wheelhouse catwalk one can watch it and see the wheel inside...the sound, the movements HOW THERAPEUTIC and what power the little Wandle generates...and all round are the detached and semi-detatched in their ugliness and dusty roofs... no colour, no style...

He gazed out of the window and then rummaged in his pocket.

"The complex is called Merton Abbey Mill. I kept a page of the local paper for you with photos and a phone number... I have lost it!... But now, alas dear colleagues; the beautiful day is passing, and to that great city we must return. Our bus is waiting."

He shepherded his charges towards the door, firmly collecting up several disorientated wanderers.

"And now we tell our friends what a wonderful day we have had!"

This took a long time. There were smiles and sighs and innumerable handshakes, repeated over and over again. The farewells seemed to take almost as long as the rest of the visit. Eventually the minibus was filled.

"It has been so good," said Helmut, followed by the observation, remarkable considering everything that had not actually happened, "To participate in creative work is food for the hungry mind of Man."

He climbed into the bus beside Paula. George started up the engine. Hands fluttered and some people smiled. Others looked wistfully ahead. The bus departed, leaving a strange silence behind. What did it all amount to? What had these intelligent, disorientated people taken in? Was this expedition any help in re-connecting the mysterious master-switch in the mind?

A switch in my own mind must have flipped too. Just now it all seemed a game, as if Helmut had imagined us into existence along with Liebermann and the Wandle and the Happy Hessians, and the games-board was now being folded up, the pieces put back into their box.

Yet we were still 'happening'. Or were we imagining each other? Or perhaps all of us, Helmut and the patients included, were being imagined by someone else and we would fade away as soon as the curtain came down and the play ended. How long then will the play be remembered? Does a play still exist once it has been forgotten? All that remained certain was the warm feeling in my heart for Helmut and his party, and for the potters, who had all done their best. Real or unreal, we were in it together.

It was too late to ask Helmut's opinion about all this. He might not have had one; his way of thinking was more down to earth. That was part of the therapy.

This was the first of several Helmut visits and it led to a warm friendship. I came to admire more and more his rapport with his people and the way he helped them regain their self-esteem. It was all so natural and so odd. He gave them so much, but he needed them almost as much as they needed him. He was a dedicated therapist and a natural artist, and though he made numerous paintings, drawings, pots, models and mosaics, his best medium was humanity itself.

Bowl, ACS 1980, incorporating three movements, inwards, outwards and around.

30

CENTERING

Michael Cardew's grave is in the field below the old church at St Breward on the edge of Bodmin Moor, a couple of miles from his kiln at Wenford Bridge. At the funeral it was cold, wet and windy, an elemental February day. At the burial, Mariel his wife scattered a handful of earth into the open grave. 'A gesture of acceptance', she called it. Most of us did the same as we filed past. It was an appropriate ceremony for one who, in spite of his complex nature, or perhaps because of it, liked to call himself a mud-and-water-man'.

Earlier, during the service, someone read from *Ecclesiastes* the passage Michael himself might have chosen:

> To everything there is a season, and a time to every purpose under the heaven; A time to be born, and a time to die; a time to plant, and a time to pluck up that which is planted.[19]

He was eighty-four when he died. I don't think the prospect of death ever disturbed him; he accepted the framework of life and the pattern of the seasons wholeheartedly and he knew very well that time was closing in. He had a shrewd sense of timing in everything he did, and I doubt if even his sudden death took him unawares.

Everyone and everything has to 'keep time'. The whole universe unfolds in time. It is the invisible dimension in all that exists. For a potter like Michael, for whom the wheel was the essential means of forming clay, time is touchable. "When you're in time with the clay you know it's alive," he once said. "Never mind what people tell you about matter being dead. They never had the luck to know any better. Keep time with the clay and the magic begins."

There are other time-keepings too: the drying time of the hardening vessel, the timing of the brush-stroke, the maturing-time of a glaze, the firing-time of the kiln. Michael knew about them all, though being an impatient man he didn't always wait and had to pay the penalty, but as a result he regarded time with even greater respect. Mud-and-water-man served him well as a catch-name, but he was just as much a time-and-movement man. After all, he was also a musician.

However closely one knows another person, when the last day comes one buries a mystery, seeing their time only from the outside, knowing that the inward summing-up must be different. Successful phases in their career may have mattered little to them, while brief encounters and moments that passed in a flash remained potent for years to come.

As we threw handfuls of wet earth into Michael's grave I became aware that we were not all paying our respects to the same person; we were thinking of the man we had walked and talked with, played or worked with, listened to or learned from, drunk with or imagined, and while he himself was all of these, most of them anyway, he was also something other. It may be only at the last moments of life that all its elements come together in their proper value.

It is said that at the point of death a person sees their entire life as a whole, not as a sequence in passing time but with every moment clearly present all at once. It is believable because almost everyone has a number of previews, moments at which time seems to stand still and the situation stands out clearly, not in relation to other events but as if fixed under the eye of eternity. English has no words for these different aspects of time, but the Greeks distinguished between them. They used the word *chronos* for time as a sequence of events, and *kairos* for time as a clear-cut moment. As a classical scholar and as a potter, Michael knew about them both.

Clay on the potter's wheel illustrates the idea clearly, for within the spinning lump, whatever form it assumes, is a central point that does not move. Every particle in the vessel and every detail of the form relates to that centre; without it they could not be where they are. Seen from that centre everything is all there equally and at once.

We shall never know whether a dying man actually does see his life as a whole until we find out for ourselves, though there is a good deal of evidence to support the idea from clinical records of near-death and out-of-the body experiences. Not long ago I was fascinated by something said at a conference by the great brain surgeon Sir John Eccles. Having discussed the immense complexity of the dendrons and dendrites and synapses of the brain by which outer impressions are registered, together with the inner memories, thoughts and emotions, he explained that all these were mechanisms of consciousness, not consciousness itself. "Consciousness resides here", he said, pointing at a central area on his diagram. "This part of the brain has no mass and it consumes no energy. Therefore it cannot die".

His words reminded me of the motionless centre of the spinning clay, which, being a point, has no mass. "Except for the point, the still point," Eliot wrote in *Burnt Norton*, "there would be no dance."

When I first read T.S. Eliot's *Four Quartets* I was captivated by the images and the rhythm and music of the words. Only slowly did I begin to realise that it is all about time and timelessness, about *chronos* and *kairos*. Then I began to understand why Eliot was fascinated by pottery and used it in his imagery. In pots he saw movement and stillness, time and timelessness, tangibly fused together.

> Only by the form, the pattern,
> Can words or music reach
> The stillness, as a Chinese jar still
> Moves perpetually in its stillness.[20]

In Eliot's play *The Confidential Clerk* the main character says he would really like to have been a potter. He regards pots as "an escape into living". I think Eliot was speaking for himself and that the paradoxical saying conveys his awareness that in every vessel thrown on the wheel, movement and stillness coexist, as one. Makers of pots actually feel this coexistence when the crude clay lump is centred on the wheel and expands into a moving form: centering the clay, the maker also begins to become centered. No amount of willing or thinking can reach the stillness of the centre, but the action can.

It can be left at that, a pleasant state of attentive relaxation, an end in itself. But it could also be the beginning of something very much greater.

Most potters would recognise what Eliot meant, but they certainly don't always perceive a perfect ceramic form as he did, "moving perpetually in its own stillness". They may be dulled by over-familiarity, and they may simply be reckoning the pot as part of a quota or wondering how to price it. Nor do they always feel as Keats did beside the Grecian Urn,

> Thou, silent form, dost tease us out of thought
> As doth eternity.

"Philosophy and that," said the practical Edgar, "it gets you nowhere".

It was fair comment, for centering, with all its implications, is something that can't easily be thought about while it is happening. A potter who was here some years ago deliberately tried to keep his mind on it, and he was a pain to work with. The trouble is, you can't catch the moment by stopping or thinking; in the nature of things, it's already gone. You only make a mess of whatever you're meant to be doing.

The stillness within which things move perpetually often comes unexpectedly and sometimes in unpropitious circumstances. A friend of ours encountered it in the war, after his bomber had been hit during a night raid and he was parachuting through intense anti-aircraft fire. Many times and many places face the world's end, and often they turn out to be not an end at all but the threshold of a wider world, always present, but hitherto unnoticed.

A remarkable desciption of centering comes in Pasternak's *Dr. Zhivago*, The episode occurs in the middle of the Russian civil war. After several traumatic months Yury and Lara and their small daughter find a period of peace in a remote farmhouse. Heavy snow has fallen. Lara and the girl are asleep and he begins to make careful copies of some of his earlier poems, improving them as he goes. Gradually he gets into his stride and starts a new poem, which takes possession of him and he becomes inspired. At such moments, says Pasternak, the motive force no longer resides in the artist.

> Language, the home and dwelling of beauty and meaning, itself begins to think and speak for man and turns wholly into music by the momentum of its inward flow. Then, like the current of a mighty river polishing stones and turning wheels by its very movement, the flow of speech creates in passing, by the force of its own laws, rhyme and rhythm and countless other forms and formations, until now undiscovered and unnamed.[21]

A whole cosmology is implied in the simple process of centering. Clay turning on the wheel is a universal symbol which relates to every human being, past, present and to come, indicating that everything experienced in passing time depends on a centre of consciousness that witnesses and remembers it all. The potter's wheel is, of course, only one amongst many wheels, but it is specially significant because there one actually touches the point in the centre where there is no movement. One of the most striking interpretations of the wheel was written down twelve centuries ago by St. Abba Dorotheus. The terminology is quite different from Pasternak's but the meaning is similar. He imagines a circle with rays going out from the centre.

CENTERING

> Suppose now that this circle is the world, and the very centre of the circle, God, and the rays are the paths of men's lives... Then in so far as they move inwards within the circle towards its centre, wishing to come near to God, then, in the degree of their penetration, they come closer both to God and to one another.[22]

This doesn't mean that the potter's wheel provides a special ticket to eternity, but it does mean that those who work with it have the daily use of an extraordinary and universal symbol. There are many other symbols, but this must be one of the simplest.

> At the still point of the turning world. Neither flesh nor fleshless;
> Neither from nor towards; at the still point,there the dance is,
> Where past and future are gathered. Neither movement from nor towards,
> Neither ascent nor decline. Except for the point, the still point,
> There would be no dance, and there is only the dance.[23]

When I was learning to make bowls on the wheel I was taught to begin each movement by taking the inside hand back to the centre of the clay and working outwards from it, slowly increasing the pressure as I shaped the side, allowing the centre to expand into the whole form. At the time it seemed to be simply a useful technique and I did not see what it meant. It was one way of describing the transition from the still point back into the "turning world" of events in time. No-one can hold on to the still point, but it can expand. Then it remains in the midst of the dance, uniting the events of passing time with a centre which is always present. Nothing has changed but everything is new. It is one of the oldest and one of the most surprising of all human experiences, one of the most intimate and one of the least personal. Lacking adequate words, one feels 'this is it.' Blake, of course, expressed it better:

> If the doors of perception were cleansed, everything would appear to man as it is, infinite.[24]

When the rain fell on Michael's coffin, and the wind blew, and we threw our handfuls of earth into the grave we were acknowledging not simply the death of a friend, but recognising the way things are, the way past and future are gathered at the still point, the sound and the silence, the planting and the plucking up, the seasons and the times appropriate to all things under the sun. And having buried Michael's mobile body, we left him in the centre of his wheel.

Dish – ACS, 1987. "The eternal gardener's leaves, enleafing everything..." from Dante, Paradiso, XXVII, 64-6

"Le fronde onde s'infronda tutto l'orto
 de l''ortolano etterno, am'io contanto
 quanto da lui a lor di bene e porto."

31

ENVIRONMENT

Aldermaston itself has not changed much since I was a child, but its circumstances have. We grew up by lamp and candlelight, for there was no electricity until 1949, and there were as many cows in the street as cars. Today its name is familiar because of the Atomic Weapons Establishment two miles to the South. This seemed to me a necessity during the period of the cold war, terrifying though it was, and still is, though most of the potters in the country protested ardently against it. Four miles to the west you come to Greenham Common, the former Cruise Missile base. To the north are companies specialising in heavy-duty electrical cables and in the commercial development of isotopes. A few miles to the east are bunkers for the storage of oil in case of national emergency and industrial estates and business parks are being developed along the once green Kennet Valley. Yet here in the middle of it all are the potters, keenly sensitive to pollution issues, supporting conservation projects and everything that is environmentally friendly.

Like most other makers and artists, potters identify themselves with the conservation of the natural world and we tend to feel that our work is innocent of pollution. And so it is, compared with industry and modern farming, and the world of high technology that surrounds us. Most of us are more interested in the quality of life than in economic growth, and we tend to regard the developers as a threatening, alien breed. It is easy to forget that most of our friends and families are involved up to the neck in some aspect of development. That's where big money comes from; that's what creates employment. We regard ourselves as environmentalists, wedging clay, drawing it up on the wheel, painting the vessels, feeding the flames of the kiln with off-cut wood, and working in conditions which are pleasant enough even though they are not overfull of comforts. We value the natural environment and feel that it has nothing to fear from us. It is 'they' to the north, south, east and west who are threatening it.

But misgivings arise as soon as we look closer. What about the raw materials for the glazes, the frits, which consist of materials fused at white heat into a glassy mass, which is then broken up and ground in vast porcelain-lined mills to the powder-form in which we use it? The natural minerals too, kaolin, felspar, dolomite, have been similarly ground after being quarried out of scars in the landscape and transported in giant vehicles for processing in factories. And then the clay, which was once dug by men with spades, an unenviable job, is now quarried with cranes and bulldozers, then purified in massive cast-iron presses powered by hydraulic pumps, consolidated in giant extruders, and finally transported by road or rail and stored in plastic. Yet how distant this technology seems when the potter takes the clay in the palm of the hand to make a cup or a curving handle.

Of course the same principles apply not only to pottery but to all the arts generally. The sculptor's stone or bronze, the print-maker's inks, the glass-blower's 'metal', the painter's colours, all depend on industrial technology and involve some degree of pollution. The intensive, personal labour by which they were produced in ages past is no longer relevant. Even in those days the earth was to some degree ravished for art's sake. An illuminated manuscript is animal skin inscribed and embellished with colours fixed by siccatives from boiled bones, stitched and bound with leather and highlighted with gold obtained from God knows where or by what means.

Almost any activity one can think of exploits the environment in some way or other, even where it is least evident: the poet needs paper and a publisher; the dancer and the singer don't directly consume materials but they need a theatre and light and publicity and transport and telephones, and these things depend on raw material and heavy manufacture and power. Even people who resolutely pursue their craft or art as far as possible independently of industrial technology still need buyers, and this links them to the source of the buyers' money, most of which originates in the very world they deplore. One of the potters here, a very alternative society girl, worked diligently on a commission for a charming, fanciable man, only to discover when it was all praised and paid for, that he was a nuclear weapons physicist. And another potter, a vegetarian, completed a dinner-service for a man who turned out to be a butcher. The transfer of money makes the world a network, and we are all in it.

Good environmentalists would like to limit their consumption to renewable resources and to avoid exploitation in all its forms, but is that really possible? You avoid using coal and turn on the electricity; you refuse beef but wear leather shoes; you fetch your organically grown vegetables by car, and so on. I suppose most people who have any freedom of choice reflect an awareness of environmental issues in some aspect of their personal life and draw the line somewhere, but none of us can contract out of the act as a whole. We would be lost without the infrastructure of modern society. Our personal scruples seem pathetic beside global concerns such as nuclear waste, acid rain, industrial and agricultural chemicals, the scourge of poverty and the destruction of the rain forest.

In the words of Dr. Boutros Ghali at the Rio Earth Summit, 1992, "The earth is sick from under-development and sick from excessive development."

So are the environmentally-minded people, such as these potters, therefore hypocritical? Or simply naive? Perhaps a little of both, but that doesn't invalidate their convictions, nor make their positive efforts null and void. All these feelings and restraints arise from caring about our world and the quality of life it supports, be it a positive love or a fear of retribution, and whatever action is taken or rejected begins first in the mind. All the arts grow from a delight in some aspect of the natural world, a reverence for it, a desire to explore it, play with it, participate in it, whether it be stone, clay, sound, colour, landscape or the forms and structures of living organisms. The arts would simply not exist if these responses weren't bedded into human nature. They wouldn't continue if it were not for the desire to extend our awareness of all these things. In the long run the arts provide some of the firmest support and the best publicity there could be for environmental issues. By drawing the minds and the hearts of men towards the given qualities of our world, the arts reinforce whatever practical steps can be taken to conserve our planet and the film of life on its surface.

It goes further, this line of thought, because whatever we human beings perceive or understand of the world isn't fixed. It depends on the width of our perception, on the intensity of experience, the way we add it up and the use we put it to. We are beginning to understand better the saying that science and art, philosophy and religion belong together as one. That is, they are all facets of a full appreciation of existence, and the further any of them is followed towards its limits, the more closely it touches the others. They all reflect the interchange between mankind and the world around him. And isn't that where environmental awareness begins? If one really pursued all the current issues, one would find they are concerned not only with the endangered species, poverty, the exploitation of resources, toxic waste, industrial pollution, and so forth, but with man himself, individually, body and soul.

It's easy to suppose that the crucial areas are always somewhere else. In the olive groves of Andalucia or the lakeland forests of Lapland the hazards of industrial pollution seem like a distant nightmare, and in trim suburbs the menace of industrial exploitation is easily forgotten. Yet working here at Aldermaston we are forcefully reminded every day that pots and poems and the beautiful aspects of land and water can no more be separated from the rest of the world than day from night. And though other people's villages are not rumbled by industrial transport and their night sky does not glow with security lights over the research laboratories, they encounter this other world in the newspaper and on the radio instead of on the doorstep. Only of course it isn't another world: it's a different face of the same one.

32

FINALE

And then, for us, in May 1993, the making came to an end. The event was not of our choosing. It was determined by the economic recession. There was no room for debate: it was only a matter of finding the right moment and the best way to wind things up.

The workshop could not have continued in the same form for ever and ever. People and places, motives and ideals, flourish for a while and gradually change. A similar enterprise starting today would develop differently and would have to take into account a very different economic environment. It was not evident to me at the time, but the expansive economy of the 'fifties and 'sixties was a fortunate moment to launch a new enterprise. It offered wide margins of error which supported the optimistic and informal way we organised ourselves. Anyone who started anything at that time had more than a sporting chance. As an economist friend told me when it was all over, "Anyone who couldn't make a go of it in those days needed his head examined."

Now the team of potters had to be dispersed, but no one was going to be lost. No-one would ever have come here looking for a predictable and easy going life in the first place. We were adaptable and self-reliant people, and we had learnt a great deal over the years, about design and materials, skills of hand and heart, techniques, prices, trading and so forth, but over and above these we had learnt about collaboration. However beneficial it may be, it is not a prop. It develops out of each individual's resourcefulness and generosity of mind. It builds people up, enables everyone to be more fully themselves, and helps people to stand on their own when the time comes. No member of the current team was likely to disappear. The life we shared was coming to an end, but sooner or later new impulses arise in place of old ones. Rather than try to hold on, losing momentum as the years went by, it was better to finish in style, to hold a big exhibition, to arrange some ceremony and a party of celebration.

In the following days it was natural to look back and try to see the past forty years in perspective. When I first learnt to throw on the wheel I had been inspired by Bernard Leach's *A Potter's Book*. No one ever more vividly conveyed the lure of making and the thrill of the transforming effect of fire. His writing undoubtedly played a part in drawing me and many others into ceramics. He communicated his convictions to a wide public and all of us who came later benefitted from an undercurrent of informed interest which scarcely existed when he began.

Leach's style and many of his values were already being attacked when I was in my twenties. The pendulum is bound to swing. None the less, his belief in the co-operative workshop, and in pottery for both use and inspiration, transcending differences of social background, seemed to me entirely valid. The way he wrote about making and firing pots enabled me to see the ceramics of the present and of past ages as diverse expressions within one vast and infinitely varied family.

Viewed on that scale, the output of the present day inevitably occupies a modest place. The arts are an activity in which there is no sign of evolutionary development such as we take for granted in medicine, agriculture, aeronautics or computer technology. The best pots, poems or music of today are not in an absolute sense better than those of long ago; they reflect another era and they are naturally simply different. All arts make use of the technology of their time, but their motivation and their impact resides in human sensibilities, joy, comfort, horror, humour, grief, compassion, insight and above all in the transformation of common materials into new meanings and new forms.

The arts have never been mainstream like the pursuit of wealth or politics or military power. They fill gaps in between the pillars of society and the conditions have sometimes been uneasy. Yet they contribute immeasurably to the quality of life and they are apt to survive long after empires have passed into oblivion. The urge to make and express is as old as the hills and for a brief span of time we played a minute part in the age-old fraternity of makers. Even if all that we made were destroyed or discounted in a few years' time, the activity itself had a value, as it has always had. It was challenging and sometimes exhilarating; we shared many good times and a few dismal ones and it brought us face to face with ourselves and with basic attributes of the world to which we belong.

At one o'clock on Saturday 29th May the sign that swung over the door was taken down and Aldermaston Pottery came to an end. It was a serious moment, leavened by

FINALE

some light suspense. The sign had been up so long that it was difficult to detach the bolts. An array of increasingly menacing tools had to be sent up the ladder before they could be undone. At last the sign came down, the wall was bare, and the onlookers dispersed. Not for the last time, some of us were remembering the old words,

> To everything there is a season, and a time to every purpose under the heaven: a time to be born, and a time to die; a time to plant, and a time to pluck up that which is planted...

NOTES

1. R. Lightbown and A. Caiger-Smith, *The Three Books of the Potter's Art* of the Cavaliere Cipriano Piccolpasso, London 1980, p.90
2. A. Caiger-Smith, *Lustre Pottery*, London 1985, p. 208
3. Condensed from M. Cardew, "The Fatal Impact", Ceramic Review no.55 (1982) p.5
4. Edward Lucie-Smith, *World of the Makers*, London and Toronto 1975, p. 55
5. Alison Britton in The Maker's Eye, Catalogue of Exhibition at the Crafts Council, London, 1981, p., 16
6. "The Use of Scanning Electron Microscopy in the Technological Examination of Ancient Ceramics" by M.S. Tite, I.C. Freestone, N.D. Meeks and M. Bimson, no. 10 in *Archaeological Ceramics*, Smithsonian Institute Press, Washington D.C., 1982
7. "Firing transformations of mixtures of clays containing illite, kaolinite and calcium carbonate used by ornamental tile industries" by F. Gonzalez-Garcia, V. Romero-Acosta, G. Garcia-Ramos and M. Gonzalez-Rodriguez of the University of Seville: Applied Clay Science, 5, 1990, pp. 361-375, published by Elsevier Science Publishers B.V., Amsterdam
8. E.H. Gombrich, *The Sense of Order*, Oxford 1979
9. From Antonio Machado, *Poesias: Campos de Castilla XIX*, "Caminante, son tus huellas el camino, y nada mas..."
10. William Morris, Lecture at The Working Men's College, London, 10 December 1881, published 1899
11. Owen Jones, *The Grammar of Ornament* (1856), republished by Omega Books Ltd, London 1986
12. Richard Long, *Walking in Circles*, Catalogue of Exhibition, South Bank Centre, London, 1991
13. From Johnson's Letter to Lord Chesterfield, 7 February 1755
14. *The Book of Suger, Abbot of St-Denis*, Trans. E. Panofsky, Princeton 1946
15. Sir David Brewster, *The Life, Writings and Discoveries of Sir Isaac Newton*, Edinburgh 1855, Vol.II, p. 407
16. *The Fall of Hyperion* lines, 198-202
17. *The Woodblock and the Artist*, Exhibition Catalogue, South Bank Centre, London 1991
18. St. John, 3.VIII *The Gospel of St John*
19. *Ecclesiastes*, 3, i
20. T.S. Eliot, *Burnt Norton,* lines 62-66
21. B. Pasternak, Dr. Zhivago, London 1958, pp. 391-2
22. E. Kadloubovsky and G.E.H. Palmer, *Early Fathers from the Philokalia*, 1954, p. 165
23. T.S. Eliot, *Burnt Norton*, lines 140-144
24. *The Marriage of Heaven and Hell*